P9-DMM-151

TOM DOKKEN'S
RETRIEVER TRAINING

HE COMPLETE GUIDE TO DEVELOPING YOUR HUNTING DOG

TOM DOKKEN

©2009 Tom Dokken

Published by

Krause Publications, a division of F+W, A Content + eCommerce Company
700 East State Street • Iola, WI 54990-0001
715-445-2214 • 888-457-2873
www.krausebooks.com

To order books or other products call toll-free 1-800-258-0929
or visit us online at www.krausebooks.com

All rights reserved. No portion of this publication may be reproduced or transmitted in any form or by any means, electronic or mechanical, including photocopy, recording, or any information storage and retrieval system, without permission in writing from the publisher, except by a reviewer who may quote brief passages in a critical article or review to be printed in a magazine or newspaper, or electronically transmitted on radio, television, or the Internet.

ISBN-13: 978-0-89689-858-5
ISBN-10: 0-89689-858-X

Designed by Tom Nelsen
Edited by Jim Schlender & Corrina Peterson
Cover & Book Photography by Lee Kjos & Mark Palas

Printed in the United States of America

Dedication

To my family – Mom, Dad, Jule, Scotty, Joanne and Ron. Thanks for making this possible. And special thanks to Sam, for introducing me to my best friend, hunting and fishing partner, and number one supporter my wife Tina.

About the Author

Tom Dokken has more than 30 years of experience turning retrievers into successful field trial competitors, hunt test participants, waterfowling companions and upland bird finders. His business, Dokken's Oak Ridge Kennels in Northfield, Minnesota, is one of the largest all-breed hunting dog training facilities in the United States. Tom is also well-known as the creator of the popular Dokken's Deadfowl Trainer training dummy, which he designed to help teach dogs the proper hold on game birds. Tom and his wife, Tina, make their home in Northfield.

Contents

Acknowledgments

This book would have not been possible without the help and support of a lot of people to whom I am deeply grateful – so many I could fill a book and then some. Although many people have helped shape my career over the years, I need to single out two people who for some reason chose to take me under their wing and helped guide me along the way.

Charlie, you have been there from the beginning. Thank you for taking a chance on a young wide eyed kid who thought he knew how to train dogs, for being a mentor but most importantly a close friend.

Ron, your support over the years has meant more to me than you will ever know. I am grateful for all the opportunities you have given me. Thank you for your trust and friendship.

To my staff past and present, thank you. Your dedication and love of what you do shows every day.

Lee and Mark, this book is truly a work of art. I am lucky to be surrounded by the best.

Introduction

This book is meant to help you from the day you decide to bring home a new puppy with the expectation of training it be a finished hunting retriever. You have a big challenge ahead, but you also have a lot of help available to you. There is more knowledge about dogs and dog training, and more and better equipment available to you, than ever. My goal in these pages is to help guide you through the process.

These are exciting times in retriever training. With techniques such as play training and early conditioning to positive stimuli, a 3-month-old puppy can learn much more than anyone would have thought it was capable of only a couple decades ago. By moving away from old "standards," such as waiting until a dog is near adulthood to begin training, today's retriever trainers are producing excellent dogs more quickly and at younger ages.

But some things never change. A trained retriever is still the ultimate conservation tool. A duck that falls in head-high cattails or a pheasant that hits the ground running won't likely end up in your hand without the help of a good retriever. And when it's a dog that you trained yourself, the reward is all the sweeter.

I want to help you reach that reward. The techniques and concepts I'm presenting here are not difficult, but you do have to follow them in order. By the final chapter, you will have a retriever that will obey your commands on- and off-leash, retrieve birds to hand, remain steady to shot, quarter and flush upland game, find downed birds and take hand signals.

You will have challenges, and there will be times when you might have to go back and re-read parts of some chapters. In fact, I encourage you to use this book as a reference guide; it isn't meant to be read in a couple days and then put on the shelf.

So, be firm but patient. Enjoy the process. Not long from now your dog will do something that will make you proud beyond words. And that's when you'll know all the hard work, this business we call "retriever training," has been worth every minute.

Tom Dokken,
March 2009

–1–
A PRIMER ON PUPPIES

The fact that you're reading this book is evidence that you value all the things that make retrievers such excellent companions and hunting dogs. Great! We have at least one thing in common. Obviously, the Labrador is the most popular retriever breed, but all of the others have their fans as well. Regardless of whether you have a golden, Chesapeake, flat-coat, curly-coat or any other breed in the retriever category, the most important characteristic that members of this group share is this: They do whatever it takes to get the job done! With this book I'm going to help you channel your dog's huge ambition so that he works for you, the way you want, and does so happily.

Before we go further, a disclaimer: Throughout this book I will often refer to your dog as a "he." For those of you with female retrievers, please don't take offense. It's just easier this way, and besides, I'm sure you don't think of your dog as an "it," do you? Thanks for understanding. Now, with that out of the way, let's discuss several factors to consider when choosing and buying a puppy. I know you might already have your puppy, but by all means finish this chapter before going on.

HIGHLIGHTS

Male or
Female?

Who Are You
Buying From?

Straight Talk
On Pedigrees

Veterinarian
Considerations

MALE OR FEMALE?

If you want to discuss the hunting ability of male vs. female dogs, go ahead, but that's not an argument I'm willing to join. The ability to put in an honest day of hard hunting has nothing to do with gender. However, there are lifestyle considerations and personal preferences to think about when you ask which gender of dog is best for you.

A major difference is that male dogs tend to mature slower than females. It might take a male a bit longer to "get it" during certain training phases. On

CHOOSING THE RIGHT PUPPY

the other hand, males are typically able to handle more pressure than females when it comes to discipline. Depending on your personality and training style, that might be an important consideration.

I have heard people say that males don't make good housedogs. I believe this is a misconception. Both genders can make excellent household companions, so I wouldn't base the decision on whether or not you plan to keep your dog in the house. That's really all the thought you have to put into this choice, at least from a personality perspective.

One more consideration, which may or may not be a big deal to you, is that a female is going to come into heat twice a year. That can be a mere annoyance, but it could also force you to alter your hunting plans at some point, and that could indeed be a big deal.

WHO ARE YOU BUYING FROM?

You may be advised to buy your dog from a "reputable" breeder. Well, what does that mean? Aren't most breeders reputable enough to stay in business? Here are some details to consider.

First, your dog should come with a guarantee on his eyes, hips and elbows. Both parents should be certified free from problems in these three areas. And so it goes with the grandparents, great-grandparents and so on down the line. The deeper into the pedigree that dogs are certified free of health issues, the better.

No matter how good the gene pool, occasionally problems crop up for no apparent reason. Hip dysplasia, for example, can show up in a puppy from a pedigree in which the problem was absent for several generations. If that happens, it's important to understand the meaning of the breeder's guarantee. There really isn't a standard for this. A breeder might offer a replacement puppy or a refund but require you to give the dog back. Well, who wants to give back a two-year-old dog that's become like a member of your family?

Discuss these details with the breeder before you buy a puppy. Make sure you have a complete understanding of the seller's guarantee, and then get it in writing. Hopefully you will never have to go through the unpleasantness of exercising that guarantee, but you are making a sizable investment in both time and money, so better to be safe than sorry.

STRAIGHT TALK ON PEDIGREES

When you buy a puppy, what you're really buying is that dog's pedigree, which is an indicator of trainability and natural ability. I

Socialiizing your puppy from day one is very important.

Anywhere you will run into people is an opportunity to socialize your pup.

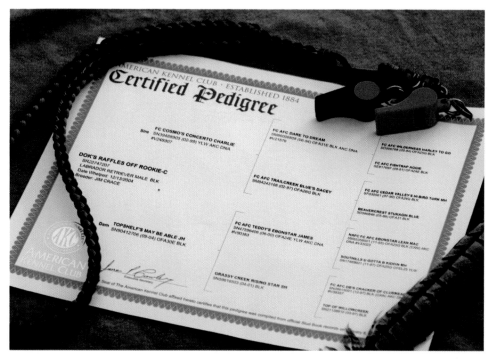

A dog's pedigree is an indicator of trainability and natural ability.

often hear people suggest that you should insist on seeing both parents before committing to buying a puppy. Unless you really know what you're looking for, or if you're shopping for some cosmetic trait (a big, square head, for example, which is kind of silly because that will have no bearing on your dog's personality or hunting ability), seeing the parents isn't going to tell you much. However, a pedigree, a written record of a litter's ancestry, can tell you everything you want to know.

Also, be aware that if all a seller can prove is that the parents are "registered," search somewhere else. A registered dog (e.g. "AKC registered") is simply one that is a purebred that has been registered with a record-keeping organization. It does not mean a dog has one iota of hunting ability. Purebred dogs that compete in dog shows are registered, but precious few of them have ever actually been in the field or marsh.

That said, there may be instance where you have seen one or both parents in action before the breeding took place. Maybe the male is a bird-crazy hunting machine and the female is the sweetest housedog you've ever met, plus a rugged waterfowl dog. And now you have a chance to buy a puppy from a breeding of those two dogs. That would be an excellent situation, but the fact is that most of the time you aren't going to have that option.

So, back to this piece of paper called the pedigree: What matters and what doesn't? If you want a smart, trainable, hard-working retriever that might double as a family dog, which is what I'm sure the majority of hunting-retriever owners want, you should look for positive indicators of those things within the first three generations. While you probably aren't looking to buy a dog for field trialing, the fact is that competition reveals which dogs have the best trainability and natural ability. Hunt tests also create a good barometer of these two characteristics, so when you're looking at a pedigree, the following designations remove much guesswork:

FC: .... Field Trial Field Champion
NFC: .... Field Trial National Field Champion
NAFC: .. Field Trial National Amateur Field Champion
AFC: ..... Field Trial Amateur Field Champion
MH: ...... Hunt Test Master Hunter
SH: .... Hunt Test Senior Hunter
JH: .... Hunt Test Junior Hunter

Of these designations, FC and MH are the most important to a hunter. You should look for multiple designations on both sides of the pedigree within the first three generations. Note: A "CH" on a pedigree is irrelevant when it comes to you picking your hunting puppy. It refers only to a bench (show, or conformation) champion. Unfortunately, some people take it to mean Field Champion, which is not the case.)

When you go to look at a litter of puppies, you do have to rely some on the breeder, who's in contact with the dogs every day, to provide some insight into the dogs' personalities. I don't suggest you necessarily go with the most dominant puppy or the least aggressive one. Play it safe and pick one that's somewhere between the extremes, if possible.

To sum up, buy the best bloodlines you can afford. This does not guarantee you will someday have the greatest hunting dog in the world, but it greatly increases the odds you will be happy with your choice.

VETERINARIAN CONSIDERATIONS

I have a major point I encourage you to think about when it's time to select a veterinarian. There will likely come a time when you'll have an emergency with your dog. When that happens, will you be able to see your veterinarian, or will you be sent to some emergency clinic where they don't know your dog? I can tell you that in such a high-stress situation, I want to be dealing with a veterinarian who knows me and knows my dog. This is someone with whom we've built rapport, and that's who I want to be talking to when I have to make a phone call for help in the middle of the night.

Other than that, when it comes to picking a vet, simply ask other folks with hunting retrievers who they take their dogs to. Some veterinarians have more experience with sporting breeds than others, and obviously that would be a big plus for you.

−2−
SOCIALIZING YOUR PUPPY

From now through the end of this book you will see an age at the start of each chapter. Please note that this is a rough guideline, just to give you an idea of the pace at which most retrievers would be capable of progressing. However, there are no hard and fast rules. Some dogs catch on quickly and some take a while to figure things out. You shouldn't be alarmed if at times your dog just doesn't seem to get it. Over time, you will develop a feel for how quickly your dog is capable of progressing.

For example, there is much evidence showing that seven weeks is the optimum time to separate a puppy from its littermates and start the socializing process. I agree with that rule. Does that mean that if you didn't get your dog until nine weeks you will have problems? Of course not. Yes, a dog older than seven weeks might have assumed a certain role in the pecking order of the litter by that point, but that should have little bearing on your training schedule.

However, whether the pup is with you or still at the breeder's place at the seven-week mark it is important that the socializing process is underway. Socialization early on is really humanization, which means the breeder has been handling the puppies and interacting with them individually on a daily basis since birth. That socialization continues now that you've brought your pup home.

With a puppy in the house you become, by default, a dog trainer – even if sometimes you feel like it is in self-defense! Your puppy will be getting into everything, from the garbage to your kids' toys to … well, anything else he can figure out how to get into. These are all opportunities for him to learn in a very short time what is acceptable and what is not. It's also a time of bonding with you and your family, and this time is irreplaceable – yes, it's that important!

HIGHLIGHTS

"Pressure On"
"Pressure Off"

Eyes, Ears, Mouth & Feet

Crate Training & Housebreaking

Treat Training

"NO"

Two Bad Habits

Loud Noises

First Feathers

Introduction to Water

Moving Along...

PRESCHOOL – 7 TO 12 WEEKS

I'm a big believer in making your retriever a house dog. Does that mean you can't raise him properly if he lives in a kennel in the backyard? In some circumstances it's just more convenient, or maybe even common sense, to keep your dog outside. But, and this is a big but, you MUST take the time daily to interact with and socialize your puppy. Again, socializing your puppy from Day One to 12 weeks in incredibly important. Do not miss this window of opportunity.

Socializing your puppy also means taking advantage of every opportunity to get him out. When you go to the bank, the hardware store, the playground -- anywhere you will run into people who want to see and talk to and fawn over your puppy – you are creating good opportunities for socialization.

INTRODUCING "PRESSURE ON, PRESSURE OFF"

When he starts to fight hold him against you. Once he's still for five seconds you can set him down.

Remember that every time you are with your puppy you are training. It starts when you are holding him and he starts to struggle because he wants to get down. Don't give in. Instead, when he starts to fight, hold him against you, and if he starts to struggle harder, increase the pressure even more by holding him just a bit tighter against your body. Once he quits fighting you, release the pressure, and after he remains still for five seconds you can then set him down. He's learning that you won't accept that type of behav-

ior. You are showing him that only when he complies will he get his way. Just think, during the first minute you hold your new pup, you have an opportunity to teach a lesson that will stay with him his whole life. You're learning something too: What kind of puppy you have and how much pressure he needs to be compliant.

I continue this exercise several times a day for three or four weeks. Keep in mind that everyone in your family can teach through this drill. Your dog has to learn who is dominant if you want him to be a welcome member of your family.

This is also you and your pup's first experience with what I call a "pressure on, pressure off" drill, and that's something I will be referring to again later on. When a puppy tries to get his way and fails, he will stop for just a split-second while he tries to figure out another avenue. In the example I just gave where he is struggling to get down, when he stops struggling I don't set him down, but I instantly lighten my hold on him. And in that brief moment, he has learned that compliance stops pressure. I can't overemphasize the importance of this concept. Soon you will be introducing other forms of pressure into obedience training, which could come via a leash, check cord or electronic collar. The type of pressure will change as you progress in your training, but the concept of pressure on, pressure off is a constant.

Speaking of collars and leashes, make sure you get a nylon puppy collar on your pup within a day or two of bringing him home. He will be wearing some sort of collar his whole life, so now is the time to get him used to it. After a week or so, start attaching a very light, several-foot cord when you take him out or during playtime.

Socializing your puppy also means taking advantage of every opportunity to get him out.

This gets him used to the leash and check cord that will later become an important part of his training.

EYES, EARS, MOUTH AND FEET

Another daily routine that teaches a lifelong lesson is for your puppy to get used to having you handle his feet and mouth, and examine his eyes and ears. Every so often, while holding your pup, simply grab a foot and hold it and rub it. If your pup struggles, keep holding the foot until he relaxes, then go back to holding and rubbing it. You don't want a fight every time your dog needs his nails trimmed or his foot examined, do you? Of course not. Get him used to being handled when he is young and things will be so much easier.

There will be times you need to medicate your dog. Get him used to you holding his mouth and looking into it. And sometimes in the field you might have to check his eyes or remove a weed seed by blowing into an eye, so spend time going through these motions now and your dog won't resist it later.

CRATE TRAINING AND HOUSEBREAKING

Probably the most important piece of equipment in your dog's life is going to be his crate. Not only will he be traveling in it, but long before that it will be where he spends his time when you are gone, anytime you can't be paying attention to him or when you simply need a break. A dog's crate is a place where he feels secure.

You should have your crate ready for your puppy the day you bring him home. Crates come in many sizes. You can opt for a small one made specifically for pup-

Get your pup used to being handled so that common activities, like nail trimming, will be much easier.

Feeding your pup inside his crate is another way to reinforce it as a positive place for him to be.

pies, or you can go ahead and buy one that will be large enough to accommodate your dog when he is full-grown. If you choose to go the latter route, take note: You will want to place a partition in the crate so that your pup's living quarters are just large enough for him to sit and lie comfortably. The reason for this is that no dog wants to mess in his living area. If you put him in a large crate, he will start using one end for urinating and defecating. Obviously, that will not help you in your housebreaking efforts.

The time most critical to housebreaking success is the first few days your puppy is home. If you can time it so you bring him home on a weekend where you can give him your full attention, that's ideal. You will likely be getting up several times during the first few nights, and you would probably rather do that on a weekend than during the work week.

Simple rule: Every time your pup comes out of the crate, you take him outside. In addition, I suggest you pick a spot in the yard where you prefer he does his business. During the first several days of housebreaking, carry him right to this spot. Eventually you will guide him to the area and it won't be long after that that he will consistently go to that spot on his own. The more often you can get him out to his spot during those critical first few days, the better.

The second part to the above rule is that you take your pup out to his spot again before putting him back into the crate. What you're trying to do is prevent accidents by creating a routine.

It shouldn't take long for your puppy to make it through most of the night without needing to go out. Obviously you shouldn't present him water for the last couple hours of evening before putting him in his crate for the night. Also, play with him and tire him out before putting him to bed – anything to help him sleep better.

As I said, your puppy will have to go out sometimes in the middle of the night. You have to be ready, so make sure you put the crate someplace where you can hear him stir. No exceptions. If he wakes up and starts barking, it's too late. It's better if you are doing things on your terms. Plus, you might be teaching him that barking is a free pass to get out of the crate anytime he wants. You will eventually develop a feel for how often he really needs to go out and how often he's making noise just to get your attention. So, take your pup out, a lot, always on your terms. Every mess he makes in the house is keeping you that much further from your goal of a housebroken dog.

Another thing I do is always feed my dog in his crate. This is just one more thing that makes the crate a positive place. However, I always water him outside the crate so I can control his intake.

TREAT TRAINING

If you've seen the bumper sticker, "Will Hunt For Food" you can probably relate to what I'm going to explain next. What motivates a dog? Food, and he will work for it! Great, give it to him – and teach some lessons at the same time. You don't need special treats for these exercises. The same kibble you feed him for his meals will work. Just make sure your dog is hungry before you start.

To introduce this concept, simply say your dog's name and extend your hand with the treat. This teaches him where the treat comes from and also helps him learn his name. After a couple of sessions, you can introduce the first spoken command to your student: Come. In a room free of distractions, wait until your pup is several feet away and then kneel down and say Come while extending your hand. You may want to say your dog's name first, but it is not necessary. Keep repeating the word as the puppy approaches and release

When teaching Come, release the treat immediately when your pup gets to you and within a couple of days he'll be running to you.

When teaching Sit, release the treat the moment his butt hits the ground.

the treat immediately when he gets to you. Do this a few times a day and within a couple days your dog will be running to you.

This exercise leads perfectly into teaching Sit. When you're sure your pup knows Come, call him to you and as soon as he gets to you, push down on his rear end. The moment his butt hits the ground, release the treat. You don't have to say Sit initially. Get your pup used to sitting before getting his reward, and then add the verbal "Sit" to the routine.

After your pup is sitting without pressure in anticipation of receiving his treat, you are ready to introduce Down. Get your dog to the sitting position, but this time, before releasing the treat, lower your treat hand to the ground while at the same time pushing

To teach Down, lower your treat hand to the ground while pushing down on your pup's shoulders.

down on the pup's shoulders. The second his belly hits the ground, release the treat to him.

Before I go on, let me remind you here that these first three commands will take at least a few days to complete. Always make sure your dog understands each command perfectly before you introduce the next one.

When teaching Place, your puppy will follow your hand in anticipation of receiving the treat.

The Place exercise is the first step in teaching your dog to move in some direction other than toward you. I like to start out teaching this command in the same spot each time. I also want to get the dog used to stepping up onto the object that I am making his place; at this stage, a dog bed is ideal. To teach Place, simply hold your hand out, moving toward the dog bed. By now your puppy will be following your hand in anticipation of receiving the treat. As soon as he steps up onto the bed, release the treat.

Kennel is just Place with a different destination.

Your puppy
will constantly
be testing
your patience
– jumping
on you,
getting into
the garbage,
climbing on
the couch …
and the list
goes on.

Kennel is really just Place with a different destination. Obviously you want your dog to head to his crate without fuss whether you are in the house or returning to your truck from hunting. Once you can send your dog to a designated place, simply repeat the exercise while substituting the word Kennel, sending him into his crate.

"NO"

Obviously, "No" is a frequent part of a puppy owner's vocabulary. It's important that your dog respects No, but early on you want to avoid heavy-handed discipline along with that word. Your puppy will constantly be testing your patience – jumping on you, getting into the garbage, climbing on the couch … and the list goes on. A firm No while removing him from the situation gives him the message that you are displeased. At the same time, it's important you realize your responsibility to puppy-proof in the same way you babyproof when there's a toddler in the house.

Here's another thing to keep in mind: Whenever you remove something from your pup's mouth, you are giving him the message that you don't want him to have things in his mouth. This is the exact opposite of what you will want later on. So think hard about how you approach him when he's got something and you need to get it away from him. Perhaps when you take a shoe away replace it with the nylon bone or toy, something you intended him to chew on.

At this point, No is more of a way of distracting your renegade pup than it is meant to be associated with heavy discipline. I will discuss more serious discipline in detail later on.

TWO BAD HABITS

Every puppy bites. Some are kind of mouthy or just nip playfully, while others actually seem mean-spirited about it. You have to show him that this is always unacceptable.

To stop this problem before it becomes serious, I hold the pup in my arms and put my hand in front of his mouth, tempting him. When he tries to bite, I grab his jowls and give them a little squeeze against his teeth. Then I do it again. If he tries again, he gets the same result but I apply more pressure.

Some puppies catch on pretty quickly, but others will test you. How your dog reacts to your discipline is a good indicator of his tenacity and how he will react to discipline later on as well.

Another aggravating puppy habit that will become a huge problem if it goes unchecked is jumping up on people. Obviously when he's tiny and learning his way around you and other people, jumping up on your leg is no big deal. But after a week or so you will want to give him some resistance to let him know you aren't going to tolerate it. Before you know it your cute little puppy is going to weigh 70 or 80 pounds, and then jumping up will be more than just aggravating. In fact, it's extremely dangerous when you're in the field with a loaded gun. Giving your puppy a little shove each time he leaps up at you, and then increasing the resistance if he persists, should be all it takes to end this bad habit for good.

LOUD NOISES

Because guns will be such an important part of your dog's life, it's especially important that he has no problem with loud noises. However, this is not the time to introduce any type of gun noise to him. That doesn't mean you have to shield him from all noises. In fact, it's good if he gets used to a noisy environment. If you have kids your work is mostly done. If you live in a fairly quiet house you might have to make a bit of noise now and then. The stereo, the TV, the doorbell, dishes clanking in the kitchen ... he will soon handle all these things without flinching.

Take care to keep your pup away from loud, abrupt noises. And if there's a thunderstorm, be sure to keep him occupied with something fun and positive. Don't give him any reason to believe that this is a potentially stressful situation. You don't want a dog that's become gunshy before he's even had a chance to hear the real thing.

Keep your pup occupied with something fun and positive in areas with lots of noise. This will help his confidence when in a stressful situation.

Introducing your pup
to feathers unlocks his
instinct to search for and
chase birds.

FIRST FEATHERS

You aren't going to work on retrieving with actual birds until your dog is five to six months old, but you can introduce him to feathers already at this stage. Get a fresh pigeon, duck or pheasant wing and use it to tease your pup into trying to grab it. Toss the wing a short distance and praise him heavily when he picks it up. Once he's excited about picking up the wing and carrying it around, the next step is to tie the wing to a string on a pole and let him try to catch it. As you tease your pup and he's showing some good interest, make him chase it and then let him catch it. Don't let him chew on it, but do allow him enough success in catching the prize to keep his interest level high.

After a few sessions with the wing on a string, the next time you're out with him for playtime simply flip the wing out onto the grass and let him run it down. All you really want to see at this stage is that he picks that wing up and carries it around. Don't let him run off and chew it up, but do make sure he gets to have some fun with it.

You're unlocking his instinct to search for and chase feathers. You only need to do these wing exercises a few times and your job is done for now.

INTRODUCTION TO WATER

Introducing your pup to water isn't difficult, but it is vitally important that you do it correctly the first time. First, find a shallow body of water with a hard bottom, then pick a hot day to go there. You want your pup to enter the water on his own, so get in there yourself and encourage him to join you. Don't be discouraged if he isn't keen on the idea at first. He is a retriever; he will

It's vital that your pup's first experiences with water are positive ones.

figure it out! The last thing you want to do is throw him in the water or, just as bad, drag him with a leash. As with all new experiences, it is vital that your pup's first experiences with water are positive ones.

Once he is comfortable in shallow water where his feet are touching the bottom, walk out deeper water and encourage him to follow. When his feet can't touch bottom he will start swimming like it's the most natural thing in the world – because it is!

If your puppy seems really hesitant to follow you into deeper water and you have another dog that your puppy is comfortable around, you can bring that dog along for a swim. It might be all the extra incentive he needs to start swimming.

Once your pup is comfortable in the water, take him swimming as often as you can. It's fun, not to mention the best way to get him some good exercise on hot days.

MOVING ALONG …

Everything your pup has experienced so far should have helped build his confidence. You want a dog that is friendly toward people, respects the members of your household and is excited about exploring new places and experiences. With this foundation, you are now ready to introduce some training into his daily life.

–3–
EARLY PUPPY TRAINING

W hile this chapter will help you advance your dog's training, it is very important that you continue the socializing outlined in the last chapter. Your puppy is still very impressionable; be sure to expose him to as many friendly people and positive experiences as possible.

This is also the stage where you will transition away from treat training. Soon verbal praise, an acknowledgement that your dog has performed a command satisfactorily, will be what he's working for. There will be times when your dog doesn't comply and the result will be a stern No! or simply no praise at all. In some cases that is all the discipline needed to let him know you're not happy with his actions.

One command, or maybe "communication" is a better word, that I didn't mention yet is simply "Okay." That's the green light telling your pup that you are releasing him from performing whatever command you last gave him. "Relax, you've done well, take a break," is what you are conveying. Your pup will quickly come to understand that Okay is followed by you throwing a "fun bumper" or two for him to retrieve, and that's as good a reward as any.

Whether you are praising your young retriever with "Good dog!" or "Attaboy!" for a job well done, or giving him the Okay when it's time to take a break, make sure you put some enthusiasm into it. Your dog is learning all about your attitude via body language and tone of voice. Give him something to get excited about!

THREE PHASES OF TRAINING

You are going to teach your dog commands in three phases that will now become better-defined than they were during simple treat training. These phases are:

1st SEMESTER HIGHLIGHTS

Three Phases of Training

Four Guiding Principles

Equipment

Transitioning from Treats to Leash

This is the Foundation

ELEMENTARY SCHOOL ~ 12 TO 20 WEEKS

Training sessions should be kept short, with frequent play breaks.

1) **Teach** – The first time your dog hears a command he has no idea what that command means. You need to teach your pup what you expect by showing him. For example, when you introduced Sit during treat training you had to push down on your dog's rear until he started to associate the word with the action. It's a simple concept, but you have to keep reminding yourself to take the time to thoroughly teach the meaning of each command you introduce.

2) **Repetition** – Sometimes a dog is labeled as stubborn. It's more likely that such a dog didn't have enough repetitions of a given exercise to fully grasp the concept. And just because your dog seems to understand a command one day doesn't mean he's going to instantly remember it the next. When you run into problems that seem to stem from stubbornness always ask yourself if you are being fair; did you do the exercise enough times for your pup to properly learn it?

3) **Discipline** – Discipline can take many forms, which I will get into later on, but the point I want to make here is that discipline isn't justified if you didn't take the time to first teach what a command means and then repeat the exercise until you're sure your dog knows it.

FOUR GUIDING PRINCIPLES

Most of the time difficult challenges are the result of the trainer not communicating clearly or consistently. Anytime a training session goes awry, ask yourself if your actions are in keeping with the following principles. Your dog is ready to learn. Are you doing your part?

1) **Keep it Fun** – Before you start taking yourself too seriously please keep this in mind: Fun first. Training sessions should not be long, drawn-out, drill-like affairs. Watch for windows of opportunity to train but always keep sessions short. And when I say short, I mean 10 minutes, two or three times a day. Furthermore, a 10-minute session might be a minute of training followed by a one-minute play break, followed by another minute of training and so on. If you overdo it, lose your cool or insist on perfection too quickly, you're going to sour your puppy on learning and that's going to be a problem for the rest of his life.

2) **Trainer Discipline** – You cannot afford to lose your temper at any time during dog training, but especially when you're dealing with a puppy. If you feel yourself getting frustrated, stop whatever you're doing and take a fun break with your puppy. Remind yourself that the reason you feel this way is not the dog's fault. It's you. Maybe it's lack of experience or maybe you simply started a training session with a bad attitude. Your four-month-old puppy did not spend his day scheming about ways to make your life miserable! So whatever you're feeling don't take it out on him.

3) **Never Give a Command You Can't Reinforce** – This is the Golden Rule in dog training. If you can't follow through on a given command, don't say it. If you tell your dog Come when he's on the other side of the yard but you don't have him under control with a check cord, and then he decides to ignore you, your first impulse will be to say the command again ... and again … and again. All you're doing is reinforcing to your dog that you really don't have control over him. What kind of problems can this create? I can't even begin to list them. Just follow the rule.

4) **Consistency** – Dogs respond well to routines. Try to train at roughly the same times each day. Be calm but upbeat every time you interact with your dog. Visualize what your training session is going to entail before you begin.

EQUIPMENT

It's time to get into the mechanics of transitioning from treat training to leash training, but first let's review the equipment you want to have on hand.

It's important that your dog responds to a whistle on some commands, particularly Sit and Come.

Leash – You need a six-foot leash. The material isn't important as long as the material doesn't stretch. I like a polypropylene leash because it's easy to work with and won't soak up water.

Check Cord – Again, I like a polypropylene material for my check cord. In this case it should be braided polypropylene in a length anywhere from 30 to 50 feet.

Nylon Collar – Earlier I mentioned getting your puppy used to wearing a collar as soon as you bring him home. By now he's outgrown that. At this stage a ¾-inch diameter nylon collar with a rugged closure is ideal.

Choke Chain – A choke chain is used to apply pressure but allows you to quickly release that pressure. This is just another form of the pressure on, pressure off concept you have been using since Day One. Choke chains come in many sizes, which is good because you will probably need to buy several between now and when your dog reaches adulthood. The choke chain shouldn't be tight, but it can't be so loose that it slips over your dog's head too easily.

Whistle – It's important that your dog responds to a whistle on some commands, particularly Sit and Come. There will be times in the field where using your voice is just not practical because of distance.

Remote Collar – No, I'm not telling you to start remote collar training at this age! Chapter 10 is devoted to that. However, it is a good idea to get your dog used to wearing his remote collar at a young age. You want him accept the remote collar as meaning it's time to go out and do something fun. So have him wear it when you let him out in the yard and take him for walks. But don't even think about turning it on yet. You have a lot to do before you get to that point.

TRANSITIONING FROM TREATS TO LEASH

If you've done your treat training properly, making the transition to leash reinforcement will not be difficult. Except for Heel and Stay, which you haven't introduced until now, the following commands are ones your dog should already be obeying with treats as his incentive. Perform all of these commands with the leash or check cord attached to the choke chain. Let's go through them while I explain how to transition to using the leash for reinforcement.

Sit – Give the Sit command while holding the treat in your hand. Even though your dog will quickly sit in anticipation of receiving the treat, apply upward pressure with the leash attached to your dog's choke chain. As always, give the treat when his butt hits the ground. Just as importantly, you must release the leash pressure

Transition from treats to leash by performing commands your dog already knows.

While holding the treat in your hand, give the Sit command and apply upward pressure with the leash.

at the same time. Once your dog is responding well, add a short whistle blast to the routine. Start out with Sit, followed by a whistle toot. After several sessions, use the whistle only.

Come – Start this command using the leash attached to the choke chain and then work your way up to using the check cord. In this case a short tug is the pressure. As always, release the treat as soon as your dog gets to you. When your pup is responding well to

Start teaching Come using the leash and work your way up to the check cord.

Come, add a toot-toot-toot on the whistle. It won't be long before Come and the whistle blasts mean the same thing to your dog.

Heel – A retriever should walk calmly next to you on command. If you're a right-handed shooter you will want your dog to heel on the left; vice versa if you're a lefty. With the leash attached to the choke collar, use short tugs to bring your dog back to your side if he lunges ahead of you or lags behind. The instant he is next to you, release the pressure. Don't try to correct with long, constant pulls; you will only end up in an extended game of tug-of-war. Use only short tugs (pressure on) and quickly release (pressure off). This exercise doesn't lend itself to treat training as well as the others, but you can certainly use treats as rewards during the early stages of teaching this command.

Down – Your pup should already be dropping to the ground in anticipation of receiving his treat. Now you will accompany the command with a downward pull on the leash. Deliver the treat at

When teaching Come, the check cord can be used as confidence grows between dog and trainer.

When teaching Down with the leash, deliver the treat the same time you release the leash pressure.

the same time you release the leash pressure. Eventually remove the treat from the equation.

Kennel – Again, your pup knows this command and is already comfortable with his kennel as his home. Give the command and guide him into the crate with the leash, then deliver the treat. Eventually remove the treat from the equation.

Stay – Start teaching Stay with the leash attached to the choke chain. Have your dog sit, then command Stay and step away. He will likely try to follow you. Be patient. Stay can be one of the more difficult commands to teach. When your dog tries to follow you, lift up on the leash and guide him back to the original spot. Command Sit, then step away. When you can do this without your dog following, and he stays put for a few seconds, step back to him and deliver a treat. It should go without saying that you should always move toward your dog to deliver the treat. If he comes to you first and you give him a treat, you just taught him it was okay to leave his spot. The goal right now is to be able to get one step away and

Create a simple platform with an old tire and a piece of plywood.

have him stay. In Chapter Six, when you formalize the obedience commands in preparation for advancing to off-leash training, you will transition to using the check cord for this exercise. Stay is an extremely important command, and you must be sure your dog is fully compliant because this will figure prominently in the next chapter when you introduce exercises that require your dog to remain on a platform.

Place – When you introduced Place to your very young puppy, I suggested you use a dog bed. Now you will want to create a real platform, which you will be using outdoors for many other exercises as well. The platform doesn't have to be huge. A simple platform can be an old tire to which you attach a 2x2-foot piece of ½-inch plywood. Lead your dog to the platform using the leash, and then deliver the treat. Once he is complying, remove the treat from the equation.

THIS IS THE FOUNDATION!

Everything I have explained to this point is the foundation for the rest of this book. Do not go further until your dog is responding to all of the commands presented so far. If your dog is beyond 20 weeks and isn't ready to go on, don't worry! Dogs progress at different paces and so do trainers.

If you are having trouble with any of these commands, review your own compliance with the principles of teaching and repetition and then review the four guiding principles. More often than not you will find that you might have short-changed your student by trying to take a shortcut. Take your time and do some retroactive training if you think it is warranted. All of this sometimes seemingly mundane stuff we call "basic obedience" is going to be hugely important when it comes to working on things in the upcoming chapters that relate more directly to hunting .

In the next chapter you are going to introduce some exercises that prepare your dog for retrieving duties. That doesn't mean you are finished with obedience training. You should work on the exercises in this chapter and the next chapter during the same time period. You can work on exercises from this chapter during one session and then exercises from the next chapter in the next session. The goal is a completely trained retriever – the whole package so to speak. Then, after getting into the "fun stuff" of introducing birds and guns in Chapter Five (during which time you should still be honing your dog's obedience compliance), you'll tighten up and finish your dog's obedience in Chapter Six. At that point your dog will have a longer attention span and should know exactly what you expect if you have been using the guiding principles explained in this chapter.

The goal is a completely trained retriever – the whole package so to speak.

—4—
EXERCISES TO BUILD ON

This chapter will help to create good hunting and retrieving habits that will continue for the rest of your dog's life. There are countless little things you can do each time you take your pup out that will reinforce these habits. Just as importantly, the principles in this chapter will help you avoid problems in the field when your dog is older.

BUILDING GOOD RETRIEVING HABITS

Although running after an object and bringing to someone is the most natural thing to a well-bred retriever, your pup will likely find some way to do so on his terms. When you throw a dummy for him to retrieve he may run away from you rather than to you, use the dummy as a chew toy, or get into a game of tug-of-war with you. Each time he gets away with one of these games your job gets tougher. Better to stop these little aggravations before they start.

First, to promote good delivery habits, always keep your pup on his check cord so you will be in control. Grabbing an object and playing keep-away with it is something a dog would do with its littermates and it may very well be a game he tries with you. If so, you will be able to catch him via the cord and remind him that you are always in control. But let's try not to go there by anticipating some of these puppy games he might try.

The easiest way to encourage your pup to return all the way to you is, after you've thrown the dummy, immediately turn your back on him and start walking or running away. Don't just backpedal; actually turn completely away. He will think you're leaving him and will race to get back to you with the dummy. As your pup gets near you, kneel down and wait for him to get

2nd SEMESTER HIGHLIGHTS

Building Good Retrieving Habits

Introduction to Casting

Hand in Mouth: A Very Important Concept Drill

Hunt'em Up

Exploring

Reality Check

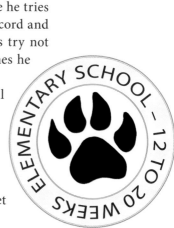

ELEMENTARY SCHOOL ~ 12 TO 20 WEEKS

all the way to you. Praise and pet him for a moment before taking the dummy from his mouth. Never lunge for him or you'll just be setting yourself up for the games mentioned above.

These principles apply for water retrieves as well. As your dog starts to near the shore, turn and start moving away. I can almost guarantee he will run you down to deliver his prize. Another way to exercise control while keeping retrieving fun is to take your dog swimming and while he is in the water toss the dummy in his direction. While he is swimming after it, wade in to a point where the water is deep enough that he still has to swim and call him to you. Your pup will have little choice but to come your way.

To keep the retrieving spirit burning, always end your sessions before your pup is tired of them. Quit before he's ready to quit, and his excitement level will be off the charts every time he knows he's going to out to play his favorite activity.

I'm not a big fan of chew toys, especially squeaky chew toys. Sometimes I see puppies that aren't terribly interested in fetching a bumper out in the yard. Why should they, when they have a

To encourage your pup to return all the way to you from water, wade out deep enough that he's still swimming and call him to you.

I can almost guarantee he will run you down to deliver his prize.

dozen of those fun squeaky toys in the house? If you want to give your dog something to chew, a nylon dog bone is a good choice for pacifying his urge and it has no resemblance to any type of object you use for retrieving exercises. Never throw a chew toy for your dog to chase. That will lead to problems later during retrieving exercises.

INTRODUCTION TO CASTING

You already have a platform which you've been using to teach Place outdoors. Now it's time to add a second platform so you can

To promote good delivery habits, keep your pup on his check cord.

introduce casting. There will come a time when you need to direct your dog to a spot from a distance. You will do this by casting, or sending, him in the direction you want.

Start with your two platforms about three feet apart. Your dog is on one of them. At this stage it doesn't matter if he's sitting or standing. With a treat in your hand, extend your arm toward the other platform and command Place. He will follow your hand, and when he gets to the other platform, deliver the treat. Then, put a treat in your other hand and extend it back toward the first platform.

Because your dog has been well-schooled in Place before you started this exercise, this concept should be pretty simple. The next step is to use leash pressure along with your arm movement to guide him from one platform to the other. Then, follow the same progression you have used with other exercises: leash pressure and treat reward, followed by leash pressure and verbal praise only.

During the next several sessions you can begin moving the platforms farther apart each time. At this stage of training, there's no need to have them more than 10 feet apart. You are simply introducing the concept. I will go into more details about extended casting in a later chapter.

HAND IN MOUTH: A VERY IMPORTANT CONCEPT DRILL

Down the road I will be discussing force-fetching. Here's a simple but important drill that will make life easier for both of you when you get to the more serious business. The hand-in-mouth drill begins with you holding your dog's nylon collar with one hand. While wearing a glove on your other hand, hold your dog's lower jaw with your thumb underneath and your fingers inside his mouth. I promise you he will not like this, and he's going to struggle mightily, so make sure you have a firm grasp on his collar with your other hand. At some point, he's going to stop struggling, even if it's only for a moment. When this happens, instantly remove your hand.

This should all sound familiar to you. It's more pressure on, pressure off, which you started the day you brought your puppy home and showed him that struggling when you held him wasn't going to get him what he wanted. Now you're teaching him that as soon as he stops resisting the gloved hand will leave his mouth. Be firm and consistent with this drill and soon you will be able to roll your hand into your dog's mouth and he won't argue at all. Why? Because he has learned that compliance is the way to get what he wants and resistance never works.

By the way, there is no verbal command associated with this drill. When you get ready for force-fetching later, you will be using the command Hold. If you've done the glove-in-mouth drill to the point of total compliance, Hold will be a positive experience with a simple concept rather than a confrontation.

HUNT 'EM UP

Teaching your retriever to search for an object is a lot of fun, and it's something you can start in the house. What's best about this game is that, when it's time to transition to the field where you want your dog to search for upland game such as pheasants or grouse, it's just an extension of the fun game you taught him as a puppy.

To get started, simply take your puppy out of the room. Then take some favorite object of his (anything other than food) and set it on the floor in plain sight. Bring the pup into the room and tell him "Hunt 'em up!" at the same time he runs to grab the object. Soon you can put move the object to spots that require him to look a bit, and eventually you can hide it where it becomes a challenge to find. Every time, as your pup searches, you're encouraging him with an enthusiastic Hunt 'em up!

Once he's made the connection between your words and this enjoyable game, move the party outside. Each time he's successful, make the game a bit more challenging by hiding the dummy in more difficult places.

EXPLORING

Chapter Seven will explain the training regimen for creating an upland hunting dog that is crazy about getting out and search-ing for birds. But here's the thing: The setup for that has to begin now. It's critical that you get your dog out to explore new places and simply allow him to roam around as often as possible. If you spend all your time tugging him around on a short leash and never let-ting him get more than several feet away, he's not getting a chance to build his confidence.

I'll say this now and I'll repeat it again later because it's so im-portant: I would rather have an enthusiastic dog that I have to reign in than one that is content to walk next to me. Bringing a wild-eyed, bird-crazy retriever under control and getting him to hunt for you instead of for himself is a whole lot easier than convincing a wallflower that he is supposed to be out looking for birds, not licking your boot heels.

So, again, please take your dog out and let him be himself. The confidence he gains will pay big dividends later on.

As a preliminary lesson to force-fetching, the hand in mouth exercise teaches him that, as soon as he stops resisting, the gloved hand will leave his mouth.

TRAINING REMINDERS

These basics apply to every exercise I have outlined for you so far.

1. The number of training sessions or the length of those sessions is not as important as making sure you are doing something with your dog on a daily basis.

2. Always have some playtime before a training session.

3. Sessions should always be short, with lots of breaks.

4. Always end on a fun note.

REALITY CHECK

Your five-month-old puppy has had a busy life so far! It's natural for you to wonder whether he's progressing the way he should and if you're doing things correctly. If your dog is responding to the exercises given you so far, your puppy is progressing and you've built the foundation needed to move on to the next chapters. However, you can't insist upon or expect perfection in anything at this point. Your pup is not going to be consistent in his responses to you because, well, he's still a puppy! Remember that. Your job is to keep on training while keeping things fun.

Your pup is very impressionable at this age so you don't want to do anything to sour him. That's why I haven't gone into any great deal about discipline. We are going to get to that shortly because there will come a point where refusing a command has to have consequences. That's how you end up with a truly reliable, finished retriever.

If you want a reality check for how you and your pup are progressing, ask yourself: Does he understand pressure on, pressure off and respond to the concept? If your answer is yes, you can be proud. You're doing fine!

INTRODUCTION TO BIRDS AND GUNS

Every phase of your dog's training is critical to how effective of a hunter he will be, but his introduction to birds and guns is an especially important step. After all, if your dog isn't crazy about feathers and the sound of gunfire doesn't get him jacked up to do the job he was bred for, everything else you've trained him to do will seem pointless. There are right and wrong ways to introduce birds and gunfire. I'm going to describe the methods we use at my kennel which we've used on thousands of retrievers. Please do not try to take shortcuts when putting the information from this chapter into practice. It only takes one mistake to turn a dog off birds or make him gunshy. Do things right the first time and you won't find yourself in the unenviable position of trying to fix a problem you never should have created in the first place.

That said, if your pup comes from good bloodlines and you purchased him from a reputable breeder, he will take to these new experiences with over-the-top enthusiasm. All you have to do is give him the opportunity to use his instincts.

INTRODUCTION TO PIGEONS

I like a retriever's first experience with a dead bird to be with a frozen pigeon. Pigeons are readily available, durable training birds. You can even reuse them if need be, provided you get them back in the freezer immediately after a training session. You will need to find a steady supply of pigeons to get you through this chapter. Talk to your breeder or folks from your local retriever club. It's usually not difficult to find someone who catches barn pigeons and sells them to retriever trainers.

If you have access to a barn, you might consider trapping pigeons yourself. All you need is a commer-

MIDDLE SCHOOL – 5 TO 6 MONTHS

Remember all the things you did in the last chapter to build good retrieving habits? Keep them in mind here. The same principles apply; you've just moved on to real birds.

cial pigeon trap and some shell corn for bait. Of course, you also need the time to check your trap each day and then a place to keep your birds. If this sounds like too much work you will probably be better off purchasing pigeons a few at a time on an as-needed basis.

I'm not a big fan of using freshly killed quail to introduce a pup to birds simply because they are kind of mushy, which encourages your dog to clamp down on them, and they're not very durable. You don't want to do anything at this point that might encourage a pup to chew, which is a tendency once the bird starts to get a little ragged after a few retrieves.

Your dog's first experience with the frozen pigeon is going to be a pretty simple one and it looks like this: He's wearing his check cord, as he always should be during training sessions, and you're just waving the pigeon around, getting him excited and then tossing it several yards for him to retrieve. You're doing this on a lawn where the bird always lands in plain sight. When he brings the pigeon back, lavish him with praise for several seconds before taking the bird from him. Remember all the things you did in the last chapter to build good retrieving habits? Keep them in mind here. The same principles apply; you've just moved on to real birds.

It's possible your dog might show some hesitation in dealing with this new object. Maybe he won't pick it up or only brings the bird part of the way back to you and then drops it. It's very important that you never lose your patience and try to force the bird (or any object, including a training dummy) into his mouth. That's a guaranteed fast way to turn your dog off of retrieving! One little trick that can correct this problem is to toss the bird a few feet into some taller grass – not into a head-high tangle of cover, but rather grass that's just tall and thick enough that your dog loses sight of you when he goes in. Standing out in the open, get the dog excited by teasing him with the bird, and then flip it into the cover. He'll bolt after it and, you hope, pick it

up. Now he'll have to make a decision: Stay alone in the tall grass, or grab that bird and get back to you, where he knows you will greet him warmly and with lots of praise.

A second trick, if your dog is a confident swimmer, is to toss the pigeon into the water. Again, this forces your dog to make a decision. Once he's in the water he can't just stay there; after he's grabbed the bird he has to come back to you. Hopefully at the very least he'll bring it all the way to shore before he drops it.

Finally, if you're really having problems, go back to the wing we discussed in Chapter Two and work some more on getting him fired up for feathers.

Keep in mind that anytime you introduce a new object there's going to be a curiosity factor that will influence how he deals with

it. For example, after introducing the pigeon you are going to advance to a chukar partridge (which I will get to shortly). That's a new and larger bird with a completely different smell. Your dog might not pick it up right away. Be patient. He's still learning, and you want to do everything you can to help build his confidence.

INTRODUCING A THROWER

Until now all of your dog's retrieving experiences have started with you throwing something for him to bring back. For the next phase of training with birds you will need an assistant to do the throwing. For the first few retrieves, hold the pup while your helper stands 40 or so yards away with the frozen pigeon. Have your assistant wave the pigeon and clap his hands, trying to get your dog fired up. When your dog is locked in and craving that retrieve, your assistant tosses the bird. As soon as your dog picks up the bird, holler, run away, clap your hands and do whatever it takes to make sure he brings it back to you and not the person who threw it.

Repeat the exercise for two or three days, at least until you've established that your dog is really excited and confident about the process. Remember to always stop the fun while your dog is still wanting more. You have to keep him on edge so he's always excited when you take him out for the next session. The next step is to have your thrower move out to around 40 to 50 yards. Important: All of your retrieving lessons are still taking place in a yard or a mowed field. The bird should always land in plain sight. This is just a retrieving exercise, not a search.

Your assistant will throw the bird and then clap his hands to get your dog excited.

INTRODUCTION TO GUNFIRE

Now that your dog is reliably and confidently scooping up birds that your helper tosses from up to 40 yards away, it's time to introduce the gun. If you have followed my advice your dog should have had no encounters with loud, abrupt noises. You are about to associate birds, which should be your dog's No. 1 reason for living, with gunfire, which is something your dog could at first construe as scary. But do this right and there shouldn't be any issues. That's why you should start off with a .22 crimp (also known as an acorn crimp) pistol, which is loud enough to get your dog's attention, but when fired at a distance shouldn't be startling. This is all about *preventing* gunshyness, which will ensure you won't be spending time down the road *curing* gunshyness.

If all has gone well, the sound of gunfire will be his cue that it's time to get excited because he gets to retrieve!

Begin with a .22 crimp pistol at a distance to avoid startling your dog.

Now, it is vitally important that you pay attention to your dog's reaction to the gunshot.

By now your dog knows that guy out in front of him has something he wants, so he should be locked onto the thrower. Your assistant simply tosses the bird up – it wouldn't hurt if maybe he angled it the throw slightly toward you – and fires the crimp pistol while the bird is in the air.

Now, it is vitally important that you pay attention to your dog's reaction to the gunshot. You already have a barometer of his enthusiasm for birds via the exercises you've been doing for the past few days. So, what happens at the gunshot and the throw? Does your pup blink his eyes as if he's uncomfortable? Does he hesitate before leaving your side? If so, those are indications that he isn't comfortable with the noise and you need to go back to several sessions of having your helper just clapping his hands before he throws.

When you are absolutely sure that your dog has no issues with gunfire and you've completed a couple successful sessions, next time have your thrower move in about 10 yards so he is at 40 yards. If everything goes well, have him come in another 10 yards for the next session. Eventually he will be firing the pistol from just a few yards away. If all has gone well, the sound of gunfire will be his cue that it's time to get excited because good things are about to happen: He gets to retrieve!

The last exercise you should do with the crimp pistol is very simple, but it's often overlooked. After a session or two of your helper tossing the pigeon while standing within just a few yards of you and your dog, have him stand next to you and throw the pigeon without firing. Let your dog go charging out after the bird immediately (you aren't doing any kind of steadying drills yet) and when he gets halfway or so to his prize, then fire the gun. What you're doing with this drill is getting him used to being shot over when he flushes an upland bird such as a grouse or pheasant.

GUNPROOFING

Now, just because you got through the initial stages of gun introduction doesn't mean your dog is ready to handle the boom of a 12-gauge duck gun. First you need to gunproof him, and you start that process by introducing the sound of a .410 shotgun. The little .410 doesn't present anywhere near the sound impact of a 12 gauge, but it is a substantial step beyond the .22 crimp. Therefore, move your thrower back out to 50 yards and repeat the same process, step by step, that you did with the blank pistol. And again: No shortcuts! Don't assume during the .410 stage that things will progress smoothly. You must keep watching your dog's reaction each time your helper moves a little bit closer. If he hesitates, turns

Carefully introduce progressively louder guns and you'll end up with a dog that associates gunfire with his favorite thing in life: Birds.

his head away at the sound of the shot or blinks nervously, have the helper move back and keep him there until your dog has regained his confidence. You might even have to go back to the .22. Watch your dog closely; his behavior will always tell you how he's handling the sound.

Once you've completed the .410 stage, it's time to run through the routine again, but with a 20 gauge. And, finally, you can introduce the 12 gauge. The introduction to guns and the gunproofing process should take you about two weeks, and that's only if everything goes smoothly. Though it might seem like a long, laborious process, the end result is a dog that associates gunfire with his favorite thing in life: birds. You have nothing to gain, but everything to lose, by moving too fast! After all the time and money you've invested in your dog it would be foolish to do something that results in him being spooked by gunfire, so do it right and you will be on your way to completing the training of a retriever you can be proud of.

INTRODUCING A LIVE BIRD

If your dog ever acted bored with the frozen pigeon during the gun-introduction drills I promise that will not be the case with his next new experience. To really bring out his desire to chase, you are going to use a clipped-wing pigeon. This is a live bird that can flutter around but can't fly away, and any retriever with an ounce of instinct will go nuts over the chance to chase one down. Remember, you have already introduced your pup to chasing with the wing drills when he was much younger, so he's already tuned in to the thrill of trying to capture something that's moving.

To create a "clipwing," simply remove the last six primary feathers. Starting at the tip of the wing, grasp each feather firmly and tug. They will come out cleanly. You only have to do this to one wing. The pigeon will be able to flutter around but can't fly away with only one fully feathered wing.

Keep in mind that, in the same way you have to watch for signs of hesitancy about gunfire, you have to make sure your dog doesn't develop a phobia about live birds. To introduce this exciting new bird, simply toss the pigeon and let it flutter to the ground and let your dog chase and catch it. A hard-fluttering pigeon could be a bit intimidating, especially if it starts flapping hard and slaps your dog in the face just as he starts to pick it up. If you think your dog might have a problem, simply tape the pigeon's wings to its body. The bird will still be able to walk and run, but can't do anything to startle your dog.

Once he's confidently chasing and catching the clipwing, you can add gunfire. Start again with the blank pistol drills, followed by the same drills you did with the .410 shotgun, 20-gauge shotgun and, finally, the 12-gauge.

Caution! I mentioned this earlier and can't stress it enough: Sometimes, when a dog hesitates to pick up a new object, whether it's a frozen bird, clipped-wing pigeon or some other type of bird, an owner thinks it make sense to force the bird into the dog's mouth to try to "show" him what to do. Never, ever do this! If he didn't want to pick it up before, he's really not going to want it now that you've caused him to associate a forceful, unpleasant reprimand with feathers. If he has any retrieving instinct at all -- and he must or you wouldn't have made it this far in the training process – he will get it! Be patient!

FLUSHING

At this point your dog is having a great time and anticipating excitement at a whole new level when he hears a gunshot, sees a bird fall and then gets the ultimate reward of chasing it around and catching it as it tries to escape. Just when he thought it couldn't get any more exciting you are going to introduce him to flushing. Ultimately you want a dog to use his nose to search for upland game and then force birds into the air as he tries to catch them, presenting you with a shot. I will cover this topic in detail in Chapter 7, but for now you are just getting him excited about the game.

To introduce this drill, go to a mowed field and have a helper hold your dog while you walk out about 20 yards carrying a live pigeon. At this point you aren't doing anything to force the dog to search cover; you are simply enhancing his instinct to chase and, therefore, flush.

To place, or plant, the pigeon, you have to dizzy it so it stays put. To dizzy a bird, grasp it firmly around the body with its head pointed down. Then, spin your wrist clockwise as if you're stirring pancake batter. Do this for about 20 revolutions and the bird should be dizzy enough that it won't immediately fly when you set it down. The bird's eyes will be open and it will be alert, but it will be too disoriented to fly. For how long? That's hard to say. Pigeons can be unpredictable and one might get away now and then before your dog can get anywhere near it. Therefore, always be sure to have several pigeons available when you go out to do these drills. On the other hand, some birds won't fly at all and your dog will swoop right in and catch them. That's okay! He just found out that he is capable of catching a bird, and you want him

Ultimately you want a dog to use his nose to search for upland game and then force birds into the air as he tries to catch them, presenting you with a shot.

Use a clipped-wing pigeon to bring out your pup's desire to chase.

When the bird flies, shoot! The first time you do this drill it's important that you don't miss.

to always believe that.

So, your dog has seen you plant the bird, and he's all fired up. Give the pigeon some time to become alert, and then give your helper the signal to release the dog. As he charges in, the bird will fly, and that's when you have to shoot it. It's very important that the first time you do this drill you don't miss. You would hate for him to think that he can't be successful in getting his mouth on the bird. You don't want a dog that figures, "Why bother, I'll never be able to catch it anyway." However, just in case you do miss, keep a clipwing in your vest and immediately throw it out for your dog to catch and retrieve. It's very important early on that your dog gets the satisfying reward of catching a bird.

Before going any further, I should mention that this drill – actually, any drill involving live birds – should take place on a big piece of property well away from any roads. If the pigeon flushes and gets away, your dog will naturally chase it. How far? No telling. And even if he's trailing his check cord, you probably aren't going to be able to catch him right away. So be safe and give yourself plenty of room to work.

GAME BIRDS

Once your dog is bold and confident with chasing, catching and retrieving clipped-wing pigeons, it's time to move on to actual game birds. I'm going to outline that process, which is simply a matter of moving up to progressively larger and larger birds. Each time you introduce a new type of bird, always start with fun retrieves while your dog is on a check cord.

When he will retrieve a dead bird with no hesitation, go through the same flushing-shooting-retrieving process you used at the pigeon stage. In a best-case scenario, assuming you have access to these types of birds, the progression would be:

1. **Chukar** – Bigger than a pigeon but smaller than a hen pheasant, a chukar is an ideal first game bird for your pup. This is one of my favorite training birds. You can usually get them cheaper than pheasants, which is nice, because you will be spending a fair amount of money getting through this phase of training. A chukar tends to struggle less than a pheasant, so getting a good plant-and-flush sequence isn't too difficult. The chukar also has a less-dramatic flush than a pheasant, so there is less chance your dog will be spooked or intimidated by this bird.

2. **Hen Pheasant** – It's very important to not skip directly from a chukar to a rooster pheasant. A hen is a bigger mouthful than a chukar but at least one-third smaller than a rooster pheasant, so it's a size that a six-month-old puppy can manage with some prac-

tice. He might need some time to figure out how to get a good grip on the hen, but that's okay.

3. **Rooster Pheasant** – A rooster is a bit more of a challenge, because it's a big bird, but also because it will put up quite a struggle if you shoot it but it still has some life in it. A flapping rooster can indeed by intimidating but, if you have worked your way up to it by building your dog's confidence first with chukars and hens, hopefully he will be showing some real aggressiveness in getting after this tough bird.

4. **Mallard Duck** – As with introducing the other species, you will start with a fresh-killed bird, but a duck isn't well-suited to be planted and flushed. Instead, after your dog is comfortable retrieving a dead mallard on land, change up the scenario by going to water. Following some retrieving drills with a dead bird, it's time to go to a "shackled" mallard. A shackled bird is alive but with its wings and feet secured. A few wraps of the wings with heavy-duty masking tape, followed by a rubber band around the bird's legs, are all it takes to ensure that the bird can't flap away or dive beneath the surface.

There may come a time as you're introducing each new species that you run into a problem. Your dog might be intimidated by the size of the bird. Maybe he gets surprised when he goes to pick up the bird and when it is still fluttering and he gets biffed in the face. If he turns off of birds or seems reluctant next time out, it's not the end of the world. Simply go back to retrieving exercises with a dead bird until he's acting aggressive and full of himself again. Then go back to the flush-shoot-retrieve exercise. Little steps, and sometimes even repeating those steps, are what's going to get you to your goal.

You're rapidly approaching the point where you have a dog that you can take hunting. That's great, but I'm going to give you another caution. This steady, no-hurry, methodic approach I have been advocating has obvious benefits during training. But sometimes in the heat of a hunting situation calm reasoning goes out the window. For example, here in Minnesota, as in several Midwestern states, we have an early goose season. Everyone is chomping at the bit to get out there in September and they figure it will be a great time to introduce their new dog to real hunting. Well … maybe. But really, is your dog ready to try to retrieve a 10- or 12-pound goose? What if it's a cripple and puts up a fight when your dog tries to pick it up? How will your dog react? How will you react? Think about these things. Your dog is still learning and is very impressionable. Be sure not to put him in situations that could hurt his confidence.

Each time you introduce a new type of bird, always start with fun retrieves while your dog is on a check cord.

Your dog is still very impressionable: Set him up for success to build his confidence.

CONGRATULATIONS!

Why am I congratulating you when you're not even halfway through this book? Because if your dog understands the obedience commands you've taught him (even if he isn't always perfectly compliant) … and feathers and gunfire turn him inside out with excitement … and he's aggressively flushing game birds, running them down and bringing them back after the shot … and he's taking to the water the way you'd expect a retriever to … and he's swimming after downed ducks like there's nothing else he would rather be doing … Well, guess what? You have yourself a hunting dog!

That's right. You have a dog that you can take hunting today. Whether it's at a game preserve or an actual wild bird hunt, your dog is ready for action. No, he isn't finished developing physically or mentally, but he understands the game and he's enjoying it. So take him hunting, but cut him some slack. After all, he's still a puppy. He's going to make mistakes. He's going to get distracted. He's going to ignore you at some point and it's going to cost you a bird or two. But at this stage, so what? Every bird he flushes or retrieves goes into his experience file and, at this age, that experience is priceless.

The most important thing is that, wherever you go and whatever type of birds you are hunting, your dog must have some success.

Now, if you are going hunting, I would prefer that you go on an upland hunt and not a waterfowl hunt over water. Waterfowling involves all sorts of new situations and equipment that I will cover in detail in Chapter 8. Frankly, it can get complicated and there are a lot of things that can go wrong. Also, keep in mind that Chapter 7 is all about upland hunting and training your dog to hunt methodically and in control, so we're going to get to those topics shortly.

The most important thing is that, wherever you go and whatever type of birds you are hunting, your dog must have some success. You can't expect a six-month-old puppy – well, any young, inexperienced dog for that matter – to hunt hard and stay excited for hours and hours if he's not encountering game. Obviously a game farm would remove some of the variables from an outing, so that might be a good place to start. Depending on where you live, what seasons are open and what type of birds you have available, a wild pheasant or grouse hunt might be on the agenda. But again, go with a high degree of confidence that your dog is going to find birds and have some success.

If you really want to hedge your bet, take some live pigeons along on your hunting trip and try this trick. Park at the edge of some light cover, take a bird, walk out a short distance from your vehicle and plant it. Mark the spot with surveyor's flagging so you remember where it is. Now go back and get your dog and walk him in that direction from the downwind side. He'll flush the bird and get a big dose of

Remember to occasionally take some time to firm up obedience.

A shackled duck is secured so it can't flap away or dive beneath the water.

fun and confidence. Make your best effort to kill the bird too, please, even though in the real world that isn't going to happen every time.

After the initial exercise, load him back up, drive down the road and repeat the process a couple more times, but each time plant the bird farther from the vehicle. Your dog must find birds to keep his interest level where it should be, and these fake hunting situations are simply guaranteeing that. Of course, as he gets older his attention span will be longer and his confidence that hunting hard will eventually lead him into finding birds will become strong.

REALITY CHECK

Now that you've done some training for real world hunting situations and laid the groundwork for a lifetime of successful hunting trips, it's important to take a brief departure from all this "fun" stuff and firm up some obedience. All those irritating things your puppy is doing now when he misbehaves might give you a chuckle but if he's still not giving you absolute compliance a couple years from now you're going to be frustrated and downright angry. So it's very important to dig hard into this next chapter and make sure you complete it, because all the confidence and enthusiasm in the world won't mean much if your dog doesn't take direction from you.

Of course, as he gets older his attention span will be longer and his confidence that hunting hard will eventually lead him into finding birds will become strong.

–6–
FORMALIZING OBEDIENCE

At this stage of your dog's life you are doing a lot of multi-tasking. He knows what guns and birds are all about now. And in the next two chapters you will involve him in new experiences that apply to real-world hunting. In Chapter 7 you will work on the finer points of upland hunting and in Chapter 8 you will get him ready for a variety of waterfowling situations. This is all fun and exciting stuff, but at the same time, in this chapter, you are going to firm up the critical obedience training you started in Chapter 3.

I can't overstate how important it is that you take the time to finish your dog's obedience training. This is really the foundation that will determine how effectively your dog will work for you – not for himself – for the rest of his hunting career.

Let's review where you should be at this stage:

1. Your dog knows the meaning of several commands: Sit, Come, Heel, Down, Place, Stay, Kennel. While he might not be totally compliant, he does understand what you expect of him.

2. He understands the concept of pressure on, pressure off via your use of the choke chain, leash and check cord.

Up to this point, you have been rewarding your dog with treats when he complies with your commands, and that has been at least part of his motivation in obeying. In this chapter, the treats are going to come out of the equation, you are going to insist on perfect obedience and you are going to reinforce commands through several different means, including a heeling stick, which I will explain in a later section.

Chapter 10 will explain how to introduce and use an electronic collar for off-leash obedience. If you are not familiar with the e-collar, don't worry. Today's models are simple to use and, if you follow these methods, you will find the e-collar sharpens up your dog's

1st SEMESTER HIGHLIGHTS
Sit
Heel
Stay
Come
Down
Place
Kennel
Refining Tool: The Heeling Stick
A Fine-Tuning Drill

obedience and makes him a more effective hunter without dampening his enthusiasm. But before you can start e-collar training you must get through this chapter. The result will be that your dog understands unconditionally that failure to obey your commands is not an option. Remember, no shortcuts! So, let's get started by reviewing each command in detail, along with the various ways you will gain perfect compliance from your dog.

The result will be that your dog understands that failure to obey your commands is not an option.

SIT

Your dog has already learned that pressure on, pressure off in regard to the Sit command has come via the leash and choke chain. Until now, when you gave the command you pulled straight up with the leash with steady pressure. He quickly figured out that the upward pull and the tightness of the choke chain both relaxed as soon as his butt hit the ground.

Now you will aim for a quicker response by replacing the steady pull with a short upward tug. With your dog at your side, command Sit and immediately tug upward with the leash. Be sure that you instantly release the pressure when he complies. If he hesitates or is slow to sit, there is no need to yell or keep repeating the command over and over. Let the leash and choke chain pressure be the influence.

HEEL

As explained earlier, you never want to get in a tug-of-war when trying to get your dog to walk at heel. You have been using short tugs along with the verbal command to keep him walking next to you with his shoulder next to or slightly behind your knee.

As with most dogs, yours probably wants to get in front of you. He may keep on trying even after what seems like your hundredth tug on that leash. The Heel command provides a good barometer of how much pressure your dog needs in many other aspects of his training. Some comply quickly; others don't. The important thing at this point is that if he's still testing you by constantly pulling ahead you must increase the intensity of the tug that brings him back.

Be sure that the choke chain immediately loosens and that there is slack in the leash as soon as he is back in position. Remember, that is the "pressure off" that is supposed to be his reason for complying. Each time you work on Heel and have to make a correction, increase the intensity of the tug by 50 percent or so.

STAY

Stay is an extension of Sit. To firm up this command, start with your dog in the sitting position, command Stay and then take one

Begin teaching Stay by taking one step away from your dog, gradually increasing the distance to 10 and 20 feet.

step away from him. He will likely try to come with you. Quickly jerk up on the leash and command Sit. Immediately step backwards, and if he tries to follow jerk the leash again with about 50 percent more intensity than the time before. Continue working at this until he stays put. Pay close attention to how much pressure it takes until he stops trying to follow you. As with the corrections you gave during Heel, this is another indicator of how much pressure your dog requires to be compliant.

You introduced Stay in Chapter 3, at which time the goal was simply to be able to take one step away from your dog and have him remain in place. It was also important for him to understand the concept when you introduced platform exercises. Now you want to extend the distance from your dog while increasing the duration of time that he will remain sitting where you left him.

Work on this command until you can back up two or three steps – the length of the leash – and then transition to working the check cord. Soon you will be able to command Stay and move off 10 feet and then 20 and so on. Be prepared for your dog to break from his position at some point. When that happens, quickly lead him back to the spot where you originally left him and start over.

COME

Your dog certainly knows the meaning of Come at this point. But does he respond without fail? You want to sharpen up his response, and you do that simply by continuing the drill with the check cord. You can transition right into this when you have good Stay compliance at 30 to 50 feet. Make sure you don't have much slack in the check cord when you give the command, and be ready to give some sharp tugs to get him coming to you the instant you say the command. The goal is a quick, snappy response whenever you call him.

Do a few sessions of this command when there are distractions – kids playing in the yard, a neighbor walking his dog down the sidewalk, whatever. The important thing is that your dog responds no matter where you are or what else is going on around him. There will be times in the field when you want your dog to come back to you immediately, but perhaps someone shoots another bird and he sees it fall but you don't want him going after it. Or maybe he's running toward a road and there's a car coming. These are times when responding to Come can't be optional in your dog's mind.

When reinforcing the Come command, be ready to give a sharp tug the instant you say the command.

It should go without saying that when your dog gets back to you always kneel down, greet him warmly and lavish the praise. You are no longer giving him food treats, but you still want him to have incentive for complying.

DOWN

Here's another command that your dog understands, and he has good reason to comply: When he dropped down before he got a treat. Now you are simply reinforcing this known command with leash and choke chain pressure, followed by lots of praise. In the same way you replaced the steady pull with a tug when firming up the Sit command, so it goes with Down. You want that snappy response, not a drawn-out pulling match.

In the same way you replaced the steady pull with a tug when firming up the Sit command, so it goes with Down.

Make your dog stay down for a period of time before giving him the Okay release command. Gradually increase the amount of time that he remains lying down before releasing him.

PLACE

To continue reinforcing Place, use the platform you used in Chapter 4. Do some reminder training via the leash and choke chain by saying Place and giving a few short tugs en route to the platform.

The important thing about Place is for your dog to understand that, once he's arrived at the platform, he must stay there until you tell him otherwise. If he tries to leave the platform, you must be there to instantly correct him. This concept will become vital in fu-

The important thing about Place is for your dog to understand that, once he's arrived at the platform, he must stay there until you tell him otherwise.

The trap you must never fall into is repeating a command over and over with no reinforcement or, worse, with no way of reinforcing it.

ture chapters when you are doing steadying drills in which you're teaching your dog to not run out for a retrieve until you tell him to go.

KENNEL

If you followed the guidelines in the earlier chapters your dog should be very comfortable with Kennel. And why not? It is his place of refuge, his home. You have also been rewarding him with treats when you command Kennel and he complies. Now you simply need to do some proofing, that is, make sure that he continues to quickly enter his kennel and stay there whenever you tell him to.

Reinforce Kennel via the choke chain and leash by guiding him inside, using short tugs if necessary. Back off a few steps and repeat. Continue increasing the distance until your dog is quickly running to his kennel from as far away as 30 or 40 feet. Remember to give him lots of praise once he's inside.

Here's one more important note regarding all of these commands: At this stage, each time you give a reinforcement or correction via the leash or check cord go ahead and say the command again. Eventually you will get to the point where you give a command only once, but for now there is nothing wrong with repeating a command, as long as you are applying pressure each time. That last part is very important: *as long as you are applying pressure each time.* The trap you must never fall into is repeating a command over and over with no reinforcement or, worse, with no way of reinforcing it. Soon your words sound like begging rather than actual commands and eventually your dog might just tune you out altogether.

REFINING TOOL: THE HEELING STICK

There is one more tool you need to add to your training regimen so you can finish your dog's obedience, and that's a heeling stick. Although this tool is very helpful in heeling exercises, it can also be used with other commands. A heeling stick is a semi-rigid rod roughly three feet long. In the equine world it might be referred to as a riding crop. They are readily available at most farm supply stores. Its use has become so common that you will have no problem finding one of the many commercial varieties in most sporting dog supply catalogs or Web sites.

The heeling stick isn't some archaic tool you're supposed to use to beat your dog. Its most important function is to guide your dog and remind him that you can quickly correct him if he tries to get out of line. While your dog must respect the heeling stick, it's

Use the heeling stick as a tool to reinforce your verbal and leash commands.

very important that you don't do anything to make him fear it. Therefore, for several days before introducing this new tool into a training exercise, have your dog get used to seeing you with it. Run the stick down his back and sides while praising him. Also, rub his chest with it so he associates the heeling stick only with positive things.

Let me give you a training scenario and show you how you would bring the heeling stick into play. Prepare to work on Heel the way you always do: with the leash and choke chain. Have your dog sit next to you, then command Heel and begin walking. If your dog moves too far ahead of you and requires a correction, tug on the leash like you always have, but also tap his chest with the heeling stick. If your dog lags behind, bring the stick behind your back and bring it around to tap him on the rear, bringing him forward so his shoulder is in line with your knee. If you need to increase the urgency of the tap, then do so; it won't be long before you will be able to see your dog acknowledging the heeling stick and accepting correction from it. You are using two forms of correction in tandem, the ultimate goal being that you will eventually get rid of the leash and guide him with the stick alone.

Remember, the heeling stick is a guide. You don't wave the stick over him or hold it in front of him in a threatening manner. It takes a bit of coordination to use this new tool, especially during the early stages when you are using it at the same time as the leash, but you will quickly become comfortable with it. The heeling stick is also a type of pressure. You need to use enough, but you should never tap him with it using any more pressure than is necessary to gain compliance. Once your dog understands and respects the heeling stick, run through the other commands your dog knows using the heeling stick for reinforcement.

To reinforce Sit, command your dog to Sit while reaching behind your back and tapping his rear.

To reinforce the Place command, use the heeling stick to tap your dog's rear while also pulling on the leash if necessary.

To teach stay using the stick, step forward, command sit and stay, and tap him on the chest.

A tap of the heeling stick replaces hand pressure.

Sit – When you are walking your dog at heel and stop, command Sit. At the same time, reach behind your back and tap his rear. It won't take long for your dog to learn that when you stop walking, he is supposed to plant it right now.

Stay – Do the Stay drill as you always have, but now if your dog tries to come toward you, hold the heeling stick across and in front of your body, step forward and command Sit and Stay while tapping him on the chest.

Down – Your dog knows Down. Pressure has come most recently via the leash, but when he was very young it was your hand pressing down on his shoulders. Now, a tap of the heeling stick is replacing your hand pressure.

Place – After commanding Place, you simply use the heeling stick to administer some light taps to your dog's rear to essentially push the dog forward while also pulling on the leash if

necessary. Perfect compliance with Place will be instrumental later on when you're working on hand signals.

Kennel – Obviously, this resembles Place, but instead of getting onto an object you are sending him into his crate.

A FINE-TUNING DRILL

There is one more drill you need to complete. It's a blend of commands your dog already knows, and he should catch on pretty quickly. This drill is designed to bring your dog to heel quickly, regardless of where he is when you command Heel. The following explanation is given as if you are a right-handed shooter who wants your dog to heel on the left.

With your dog sitting and you standing directly in front of him (so you're almost toe to toe), command Heel and tap-tap-tap him on his left side while guiding him with the leash. As he pivots around to get into the Heel position, step forward and through the area where he was just sitting. You can move pretty rapidly when doing this drill, as if you're letting him know that if he doesn't get out of your way you're going to walk right over the top of him. Once he's at your side, continue walking with your dog at heel, administering taps to the chest or rear as necessary to keep in the proper Heel position. Walk several yards and then stop. Tap his rear if he does not sit immediately. Command Stay. Step around so you are facing your dog again and repeat the drill.

After your dog is performing this drill with excellence, begin with him sitting farther away from you. Now you're really combining Stay, Come and Heel into one drill. Keep on working toward excellence.

Next, get out those two platforms you used earlier during Place drills. Set them out about six feet apart. Have your dog sit on one while the other one is positioned on your left side. Call him to you. He is already used to moving from one platform to the other. He will quickly figure out that he should do so now. As always, use the heeling stick to guide him if he tries to stop in front of you or go to the wrong side. Once he is sitting at heel on the platform, walk over to the other platform and repeat the command.

The best result of these finishing drills is that down the road when your dog is returning to you with a duck or pheasant he automatically returns to your left side and sits to deliver without any prompting from you. And that's just another example of why obedience is such an important part of creating a hunting dog you can be proud of.

−7−

UPLAND HUNTING SKILLS

The last chapter on finishing obedience began by noting that you'll have a lot of multi-tasking to do at this stage of your dog's life. You'll see what I mean in this chapter, where you are going to work on introducing and improving upland hunting skills, and in the next chapter on waterfowling skills. The activities in chapters 6, 7 and 8 can all occur at the same time. You don't have to have obedience training finished before working on the field drills outlined in this chapter and the next. Perhaps after three or four good obedience sessions you head out the next day to work on upland hunting, then go back to obedience again the next day. Or maybe have a field session in the morning and an obedience session in the evening. Your dog's progress and attitude will help you decide how to proceed, but the most important thing right now is that you are working with him on a daily or almost-daily basis.

BUILDING CONFIDENCE

Because I knew you would be anxious to introduce your dog to some real hunting experiences by the time you got to the end of Chapter 5, I gave you some suggestions for ways to ensure early success, namely by planting birds in hunting habitat or going to a game farm. That was just a taste of what would be coming in the real world. Now you're going to work on ways to make your dog an effective upland hunter by applying more specific drills to your outings.

One key to effective upland hunting is having your dog run with a purpose, not just randomly racing around the field wherever he wants. The best way to cover a field is for your dog to work back and forth in front of you. I will get to that in the next section, but first you have to fire your dog up by convincing him

---

2nd SEMESTER HIGHLIGHTS

Building Confidence

Introducing Quartering

The Value of Trailing Skills

Trailing Live Birds

Thoughts On Whistles

Dealing With Various Wind Direction

JUNIOR HIGH SCHOOL ~ 6 TO 7 MONTHS

The result
will be that
your dog
understands
that failure
to obey your
commands is
not an option.

that every time his feet hit the ground he is going to find a bird to catch or flush. For starters, take him to a field with some light cover – foot-high grass is ideal – and plant two or three clipped-wing pigeons. You don't need to use game birds for this exercise; right now you're just showing him there's something out there to get excited about.

Plan out your drill before you put the birds down. Work your dog into the wind so he has every opportunity to scent the birds. I always mark the birds' locations with surveyor's tape so I don't lose track of them and can sort of steer my dog in the right direction if necessary. You don't need a huge area to work in initially; a five-acre field is plenty large enough for starters. In fact, the first bird you plant need only be 25 yards or so from your vehicle. Even though you are introducing various components of upland hunting, success is hugely important, so always try to create "sure thing" opportunities for your dog. Therefore, keep this initial drill short and easy to manage by putting the second bird out another 30 yards or so beyond the first and the third one another 30 yards beyond that.

If you have a dog that has shown any hesitation at all about getting out away from you and searching, you could even have a helper hold your dog while you walk out and plant the first bird. When you come back, release the dog and let him run out, find and catch the pigeon. This is not an exercise about control. Its purpose is to get your dog excited about searching for game and learning to use his nose.

The first few days you do this drill, use the same area. I suggest you even plant the birds in roughly the same spots (making any necessary adjustments for wind direction, of course). You can plant fully feathered pigeons and shoot them when they fly, but continue to mix in a clipwing every now and then. Once your dog has some success, he should be going absolutely bonkers with excitement each time you head to the field. Run these drills with your dog dragging his check cord so that if he goes off on a chase it will be easier for you to bring him back under control. But even that is okay; you would rather have a dog that's bird-crazy enough to chase a bird than one you have to constantly encourage to get more than a few feet away from you.

INTRODUCING QUARTERING

Assuming your dog has the confidence to run hard and search for birds, it's time to bring some semblance of order to his upland hunting. For this next step, plant some birds randomly around the field and run your dog with his check cord on. Your dog has 30

When your dog flushes the pigeon, be ready to drop the check cord and shoot the bird.

to 50 feet of freedom, and he'll probably want to run right to the end of it. You have to get him used to running back and forth, not in a straight line, and then you have to get him used to changing direction when you want him to. To do this, give your dog an encouraging "Hunt 'em up!" and walk at a right angle in the general direction of the bird. Then, after several steps, angle back to the left. As you change directions, say your dog's name and give a tug on the check cord. Initially, you aren't giving a command (other than saying his name to get his attention). You're just getting him to respond to the check cord and work the way you want him to.

Hopefully, your dog will not run all the way back to you when you're doing this drill. After all, he's back in that familiar field where he's had all the fun during four or five bird-finding sessions. Hopefully you have the opposite problem: a dog that's borderline out of control and wants to run and run until he finds feathers.

When your dog does locate a pigeon and jumps in to flush it, drop the check cord and be ready to shoot so he can retrieve the prize. Don't be too concerned with the details of the retrieve or your dog's delivery at this point. The goal of this drill is that your dog starts to understand the concept of staying out in front of you and searching methodically.

I should also mention again the importance of doing these drills in a field with light cover. If you start working in fields with cover over your dog's head, he's going to lose confidence and probably try to stay closer to you or, worse yet, start walking behind you. Can't have that! In upland hunting it's all about building confidence and keeping his excitement level maxed out.

This drill requires lots of repetition, so get out as often as you can. Over the course of a couple weeks, increase the amount of time and distance between when you start to when he finds that first bird. Also, do your best to hunt your dog directly into the wind. If conditions don't permit that, try to work him across the wind. Be sure to not hunt with the wind at your back. There will be times during actual hunts where you have no choice, but you can worry about that later.

If things are going reasonably well at this point it's time to put a little more challenge into these drills. When you are sure your dog would rather be anywhere except next to you because he's so keyed on getting after those birds, move this drill to a new location with denser cover. This cover should be of a height where your dog can always see you but must work a little harder to get through it. This is also a good time to trade pigeons for game birds. Except for the fact that you are still controlling your dog with the check cord, these exercises are becoming more and more like real hunting.

When you are sure your dog would rather be anywhere except next to you because he's so keyed on getting after those birds, move this drill to a new location with denser cover.

When you initially make that move to heavy cover, regardless of how well your dog has been performing in lighter cover, make sure he finds birds close your starting point. You want to make sure your dog always has incentive to get into the thick stuff and aggressively search. If he thinks that busting through nasty tangles and thick grass isn't going to earn him anything he might become content to always take the path of least resistance, and that's not going to help you bag more birds.

Remember, your dog is still wearing his check cord for all of these drills. When you start working in heavier cover you may want to change to a shorter-length rope, simply to avoid having it get wrapped up in the cover as often.

The early stages of trailing practice require nothing more than a training dummy scented with commercial bird scent.

THE VALUE OF TRAILING SKILLS

Retrievers make excellent trailing dogs, a skill that is incredibly valuable in upland hunting. A wing-tipped rooster pheasant that comes down with two good legs can run a long ways. In thick cover, the chances of finding that bird without the help of a good

Give "hunt-em-up" command to start trailing drill.

retriever are pretty slim. In fact, if you're talking strictly upland hunting and I had to choose between a dog that's good at marking the fall or one that's good at trailing, I would pick the trailing dog every time. If you down a bird and have trouble finding it you can always bring your trailing dog to the area and count on him to make a great effort at unraveling the path the bird took. Dogs can become excellent trailers through lots of hunting experience, but you can move the process along by creating fun and exciting practice scenarios.

The early stages of trailing practice require nothing more than a training dummy scented with commercial bird scent that you attach to a string and drag along the ground creating a scent trail. You can use a Deadfowl Trainer and inject scent into it or you can apply the scent to a canvas dummy. Both work well and are preferable to a rubber dummy, which can't hold scent for a long time. In the event that your dog isn't terribly fired up for the fakes, you could use an actual dead bird for this drill instead. Regardless of the object, the first trailing drills need to take place in light cover, just high enough and thick enough that your dog has to use his nose and can't look ahead to see the object lying on the ground.

You certainly don't have to wait until this stage of your dog's training to introduce trailing. It can be done in the yard when your pup is much younger. Regardless of when you begin, the most important thing is to make the trailing distance short – really short, like 10 feet. Otherwise the tendency is for the dog to put his nose the ground, take a few steps and then either stay focused on that spot or simply lose interest and go back in the direction he started. As always, you have to create early success by keeping things simple.

Once he gets the hang of things, increase the distance he has to trail. After that, create curving or zigzag trails so he has to really keep that nose down to unravel the puzzle. Your dog's aptitude for this exercise will dictate how fast you progress to the more challenging drills. If he's a fast learner you might be tempted to make things complicated and try to outsmart him. Don't do that too early. It's important he has success every time. Other challenging twists to this exercise could include making your dog trail through varying types and thickness of cover.

The best time to set up trailing exercises is early morning. There will be some moisture on the grass to help hold scent. Avoid dry, windy days; these are counterproductive in this drill.

I always encourage trailing by using the same "Hunt 'em up!" encouragement I use during upland drills. I'm just letting him know, again, that there's something out in the field to find. Over

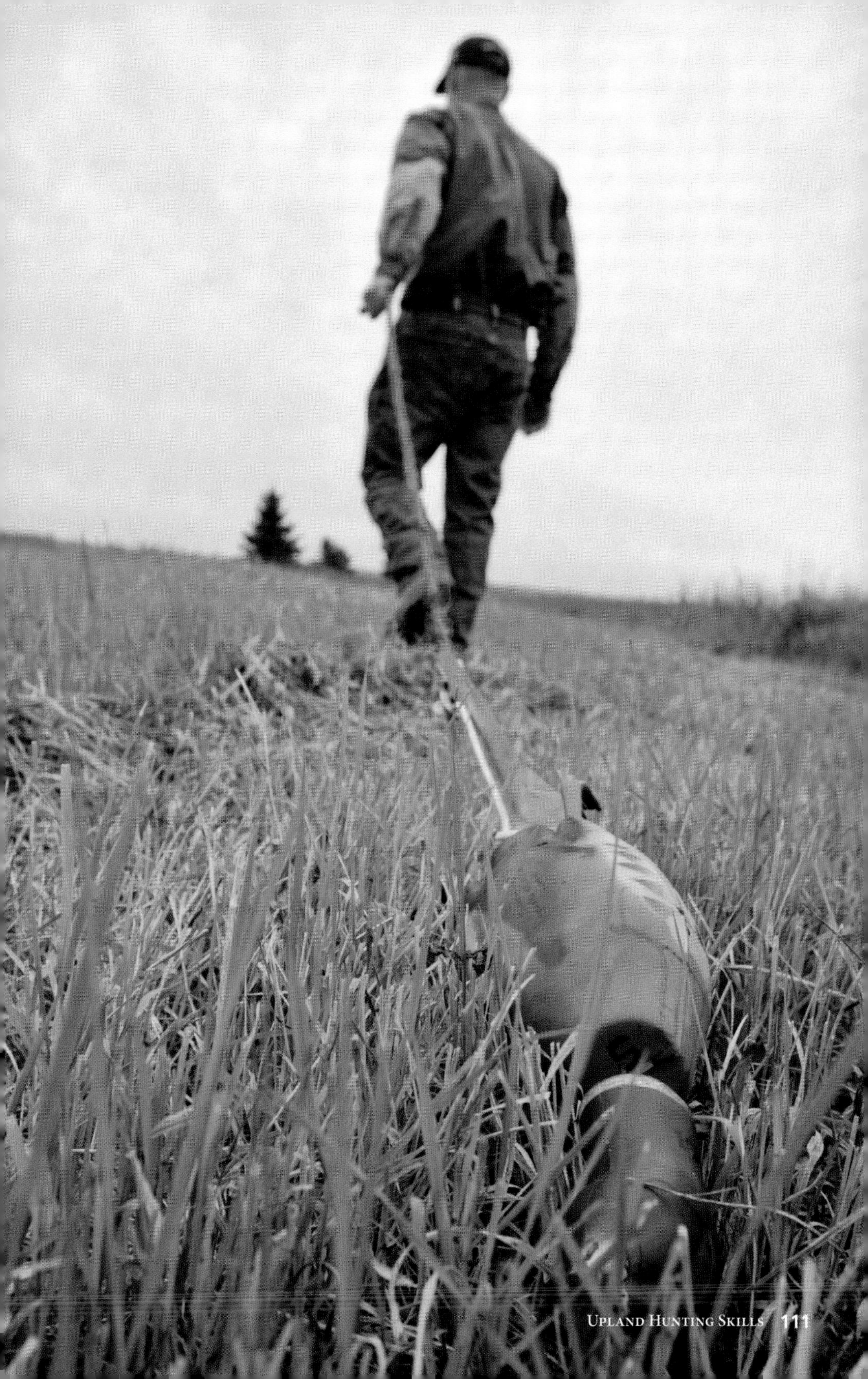

time you can introduce the command, "Hunt dead!" and keep repeating it as he's trailing. After your dog gets a season or two of experience, he will easily understand the difference between searching for birds to flush and trailing a bird that's already down.

TRAILING LIVE BIRDS

When you think your dog is really getting the hang of using his nose, set up some challenges with live birds. A pigeon with its wings secured or with both wings clipped is a good way to start. Toss the bird into some light cover and walk toward it a bit to get it moving. Wait several minutes, during which time hopefully it will cover some ground. Then bring your dog to the area where you started and encourage him to Hunt Dead.

You can progress to a chukar if you'd like, but you can't really rely on them to move any great distance. I like to use a pheasant, but a rooster will run out of the county if you just tape his wings and turn him loose. So take that rooster and hobble him by tying a string between his feet. Just leave a couple of inches so he can walk but can't really stride out and take off. As with the pigeon, give the pheasant a few minutes' head start and then bring your dog in for the search. This is a great drill, and when he comes up with a rooster that he had to trail 100 yards or maybe even farther, you have every reason to be proud of him.

You could also use a mallard duck for this drill. Even though it isn't an upland bird, your dog probably won't care. You don't have to hobble a duck because it isn't going to run very fast, but it will certainly move through the cover and provide a good trailing challenge.

One tip that will help your dog achieve success in live-bird trailing drills: Wet that bird down first. As it moves through the grass it will leave a better scent trail than it does when dry.

THOUGHTS ON WHISTLES

No one wants to hunt with the guy who is constantly blasting on his whistle in an effort to get his dog under control. On the other hand, a whistle does have its place in upland hunting, even though your dog is usually only 10 or 20 yards

A whistle doesn't have to be especially loud, just enough volume to get his attention.

away. Your dog should already understand that a series of long blasts means Come. Now you can introduce a whistle command that simply tells him, "Hey, pay attention. I want you to change directions now."

This is a very simple concept for your dog to understand. Each time you give that tug on the check cord to get him to change directions, give a two-note beep-beep on the whistle. It doesn't have to be especially loud, just enough volume to get his attention. Once he's quartering nicely, you'll rarely need to use your whistle, but it's nice to know you can give your dog a reminder now and then or get his attention without yelling. There's not much else to say about whistles. It really is that simple.

DEALING WITH VARIOUS WIND DIRECTIONS

When you hunt into the wind your dog will naturally (or at least more cooperatively) quarter back and forth as he tries to pick up bird scent. But the reality is that you can't always hunt into the wind. If you're hunting south to north and there is a west wind cutting across your path, your dog will have a tendency to run straight away from you as he tries to pick up scent. He instinctively knows that there is no point in quartering back and forth in this situation; it's much more efficient to run a line trying to pick up scent blowing crossways.

If your find yourself hunting a field or woodlot with the wind at your back, it creates a new set of challenges even more difficult than a crosswind. Your dog's tendency will be to run straight out and then turn and work back toward you with the breeze in his face, pinning a bird between you and him. While that seems like a smart way to work – and while on occasion things work out that way – the more likely scenario is that he will push birds out ahead, they will flush wild and you will go back to the truck empty-handed.

For now, just remember to always pay close attention to wind direction so you don't set your dog up to fail and frustrate yourself at the same time. Later on I will explain how to have a productive hunt and keep your dog in control, even when the wind is "wrong."

FINAL THOUGHTS

Everything described in this chapter will go much more smoothly if you got your dog out for walks and allowed him the freedom to explore when he was younger. Too often dogs won't get out and

If you happen to have a dog that hesitates to get out in front and seek game, as a last-ditch effort you can try running him with a more experienced dog.

seek birds or bust cover because their owners drilled too much obedience, particularly Heel, into them when they were little puppies. Again, I would rather have a dog that I have to reign in than one that is following me around all day.

If you happen to have a dog that hesitates to get out in front and seek game, as a last-ditch effort you can try running him with a more experienced dog. There are no guarantees that this will make a difference, but it's worth a try. I don't really believe that an older dog can teach a younger dog anything, but if your dog gets out and runs with the other dog and finds out he's having fun, well, maybe some of that attitude will rub off on him.

Those are the basics of upland hunting training. You will add more control to your hunts after completing the off-leash training in Chapter Ten. In the meantime, you have a dog that wants to look for birds and has had a great deal of success in doing so. Now we can move on to a topic that is just as exciting to most retriever owners: Waterfowling.

–8–
WELCOME TO WATERFOWLING

While the desire to retrieve a duck is bred right into your dog, an innate understanding of the dizzying amount of paraphernalia that is part of waterfowling is not. Introducing your pup to upland hunting, covered in the last chapter, is in many ways much simpler than getting him ready for a duck or goose hunt.

Now I'm going to try to give you ways to prepare for that day when you finally get to go waterfowl hunting. Opening day of duck season is NOT the day for your dog to find about the many new sounds and equipment of the hunt. Work on these things ahead of time and you and your dog will enjoy a much more pleasant experience when the birds start flying and the shooting starts.

Part of this preparation includes simple marked retrieves in water using a boat. Keep in mind that at this point you aren't insisting on perfection. You're just giving your dog a taste of working in the environment where he'll be spending lots of time later on. Chapter 11 will cover marking skills and more advanced exercises that will really challenge your dog and sharpen him up so he's ready to play in the big leagues.

2nd SEMESTER HIGHLIGHTS

Ready, Set ...

Introducing Quartering

The Value of Trailing Skills

Trailing Live Birds

Thoughts On Whistles

Dealing With Various Wind Directions

READY, SET ...

Waterfowl hunting is a gear-intensive endeavor. Your dog already knows about guns, but now you need to familiarize him with the rest of your stuff. Let's run through the list.

Duck Decoys – Introducing your pup to decoys is as simple as scattering several mallard fakes around the yard and then taking him for a walk (on his leash) through them. Some dogs are curious about them, some are hesitant to go near them and still others will

try to charge in and pick one up. While it's okay to let him sniff the dekes and check them out, if he tries to pick one up you need to quickly give a tug on the leash and tell him No! Don't overdo the discipline; you don't want a duck dog that's afraid of fake ducks.

After your dog figures out that decoys are just another part of the landscape, trade the leash for a check cord and do some short bumper tosses in amongst the decoys. Hopefully his excitement about retrieving will outweigh his desire to mess with the plastic ducks. After a few of those, throw the dummy a bit farther so that it lands on the other side of the decoys. You want him to run through, not around, the spread on the way out and on the way back to you.

If you're going to use spinning wing decoys, add one or two to your practice spread. You might even want to set one up out in the yard and leave it out for a couple weeks, turning it on occasionally when your dog is out so that he gets used to seeing this odd-looking contraption. As with the regular decoys, soon he it will be just another part of the routine.

If you're going to use spinning-wing decoys, be sure to get your dog used to this odd-loking contraption.

Next, move the game to the water. Start by putting the decoys only a foot or so offshore. That way, if there's a problem it takes place right in front of you within easy reach. Toss the dummy out and have him come back. No problems? Good. Move the decoys

With proper training, your pup will quickly figure out that decoys are just another part of the landscape.

out about 10 feet and toss the dummy beyond them. As on land, he should take a direct line out and back in. Then progress so that the spread is all the way out at 20 yards or so offshore. You don't want him to swim around the flock. If he acts like he's avoiding the decoys, move them closer and start over.

Neoprene Vest – All you have to do is sit in a duck blind on a chilly day and watch a retriever shiver miserably to understand the value of a neoprene vest. Look at all the stuff you're wearing! Shouldn't your dog have some help to stay warm too? The vest is such a simple way to keep your dog performing well in nasty weather that I recommend everyone keep one handy. The

Once he's having fun on land, move the game to the water.

When retrieving your dog should take a direct line out and back in, not swim around the flock of decoys.

*Opening day
of duck season
is not the time
for your dog to
experience new
equipment.*

vest is also a good way to gain you an extra month of training in spring. You can swim your dog in some pretty cold temps if he's wearing his vest. But don't wait until the day your dog needs a vest to first put it on him.

Pick a day that's not too hot to get your dog used to wearing his new apparel. By the way, you might end up buying a couple of vests to accommodate him as he grows. I tend to like the vests that are made out of thinner neoprene rather than thicker material because they stretch more easily. Also, when picking the vest size, make sure it fits nice and tight. The point of having your dog wear it is to keep him warm, so you don't want air space between his body and the material.

A neoprene vest is a simple way to keep your dog performing well in nasty weather.

If you'll hunt from a motorized boat, take your dog for a ride to introduce him to the hum of the motor and the rocking of the waves.

Once you can call him to you in the boat and then back out, do some simple retrieving drills in which he has to jump out of the boat and then re-enter it to deliver the dummy. When he's comfortable with all of this, move the boat to the water's edge and do more of the same. Make sure the water is shallow; you want him to be able to feel bottom when he jumps out.

The next step is to move the boat farther from shore. This is a big step because suddenly getting back into the boat isn't so easy. You don't want him to get near the boat and start panicking when he realizes he can't climb in himself. Hoisting a wet dog into a boat doesn't have to be an ordeal. It's pretty simple after you practice and the two of you learn how to coordinate things. As your dog gets near the boat, simply reach down and grab him by the scruff of neck and lift steadily. He'll naturally put his feet on the edge of the boat once you've lifted him high enough, and then he'll push his head against your hand for leverage. A few sessions of this and it will all be routine.

Are you going to use a motorized boat for hunting? If so, that's another experience he has to get used to. Simply go for a few boat rides so he gets used to the hum of the motor and the rocking of the waves.

Once he's comfortable with the idea of the boat, do some simple retrieving drills.

The Blind – Duck hunting is about waiting … and sometimes waiting and then waiting some more. If your dog can't sit still for extended periods of time, even a relatively short outing will turn into a frustrating experience for you and your hunting partners. So, yes, you have to practice doing nothing. Have a seat in your lawn chair and position your dog sitting next to you on his leash. Relax, read the newspaper and just hang out for awhile. Your dog has to stay put. It's that simple. If you can't sit and relax for a half-hour to an hour at a time without your dog trying to sneak away, how do you expect to duck hunt from a blind? Again, this is one more thing you can take care of well before your dog's first big hunt.

During this introduction, make sure the water is shallow so your dog can feel bottom when he jumps out.

Whether you're a good waterfowl caller or a poor one, your dog just knows it's noisy.

Duck and Goose Calls – Whether you're a good waterfowl caller or a poor one doesn't matter to your dog. All he knows is that your calling is noisy and startling. Make sure this noise becomes commonplace by quacking away on your call before you throw some fun bumpers. Add the blank pistol into the mix too. Then, have your helper throw some bumpers after blowing on a duck or goose call and then firing a gun.

Field Decoys – If you're going to be field hunting, you have still more equipment to deal with and share with your dog. You have those great big Canada goose shells or full-body dekes, some of which might stand taller than your dog! These can really spook a dog, especially if the first time he sees them is just as dawn is breaking. So take the time to introduce them the same way you did with duck decoys.

Dog Blind – The camo tents that many hunters use while field hunting have become quite popular. If you plan to use one of these, it's a pretty simple matter to get your dog used to it. He already knows Kennel as it applies to his travel crate. Now just get him used to kenneling in his blind. Of course, then he has to stay there, so practice your newspaper-reading drill while he sits or lies inside.

Large Canada goose shells or full-body decoys might stand taller than your dog and could spook him the first time he sees them. If you hunt geese, be sure to train with large training dummies.

Also, do some retrieving practice with your dog starting from inside his blind. After he delivers the dummy or bird, have him get back inside and practice waiting some more.

Layout Blind – Some hunters prefer to situate their dog at their feet when field hunting from a layout blind. In fact, some models of layout blinds feature an area specifically for your dog

If you'll be using a layout blind, introduce your dog to the situation to avoid safety issues.

to hide along with you. This all seems like a great idea, but it does bring up a safety issue. Your dog will be very close to the gun, and if there's a chance he's going to jump up or break when birds start working the decoys, that's a recipe for disaster. If you go this route, set everything up and get your dog used to the situation, including firing the gun and having a helper toss marks out into and around the decoys.

INTRODUCTION TO STEADINESS
WITH THE PLATFORM

At this point your dog is comfortable with the platform. He goes to it when you give the Place command, and he obeys Stay. Now we're going to insist on something new. For the first time in your dog's life, you're going to make him stay on the platform and watch a mark fall, and you're going to make him stay there until you say it's okay to go for the retrieve. This is a good time to start using his name to release him to retrieve. If he shows some confusion, mix in the Okay command until he understands that his name means the same thing. Breaking, which is leaving for a retrieve before the handler sends the dog, is an unpardonable offense in a waterfowl retriever. At least is should be! If you want a truly reliable dog that you can be proud of in any situation, you need to insist on steadiness at all times.

Thes drills can certainly be done earlier than the 6- to 7-month stage. The risk you run in steadying is that, if you have a dog that doesn't have a lot of natural drive and you lean on him too hard to stay put, you could turn him off of retrieving. Once that happens it's awfully hard to bring his desire back. Keep in mind that it's better to have a dog that you have to reign in than one that won't go out and hunt. You are the only one who knows your dog well enough to make the call.

First, steadiness is a safety issue. If you shoot at a duck and your dog starts thrashing around in the blind or boat in an effort to jump into the water, he could crash into your or another hunter. Not good. Second, if you drop a duck and then moments later have another flock working your decoys, you can't have your dog out there swimming around or he's going to spook the birds. So let's get this done.

First, do some review compliance by sending him to the

platform while he's wearing the leash or check cord. Walk around the platform and then away from him. If you have truly finished the Stay command and done a few sessions of practicing patience with the lawn chair drill, this shouldn't be a problem. If he leaves, command Place and use the leash or check cord to quickly get him back onto the platform.

Next, with a firm grip on the leash, stand next to the platform and toss the dummy out. If he tries to bolt after it, tug him back and command Stay. When he is back under control, wait a couple seconds and release him to make the retrieve. Until now, you have been using Okay to release him. You can now begin sending him simply by saying his name. You don't have to shout it or make a big deal out of it; saying his name is simply a way to let him know it's time for him to go do his favorite thing. Of course, the first time you say his name he won't know that you are telling him to go, so you can follow it up with Okay until he starts to get the picture.

Steadiness is vitally important to the development of a complete retriever, and we'll come back to this topic with more advanced training exercises in Chapter 11. For now, keep working on the basic principle that he no longer gets to go until you say it is okay.

When you get to the point that your dog is no longer trying to tear your arm off chasing every throw, start mixing things up. Wait longer and longer after the throw to release him. Sometimes you can even walk out and pick up the bumper yourself, all the while insisting that your dog stays put on the platform. Eventually you can work up to some longer retrieves with your helper doing the throwing. Mix in some of the other waterfowling gear and principles from this chapter. For example, start with you and your dog in the boat looking out at a dozen decoys scattered about on the ground. Have your helper blow a duck call, toss a dummy and fire a gun. Then wait several seconds before sending your dog by saying his name.

There is no need to start making things complicated or mess around with variations such as advanced retrieves. Again, we will get to that soon. First, we have a couple more serious topics to cover: force-fetching in Chapter 9 and using the remote training collar in Chapter 10.

–9–

FORCE-FETCHING

orce-fetching can be a difficult concept for some folks to rationalize. They wonder why, if their dog is such a bird-crazy retriever, they should have to "force" him to do what he loves. Well, let me clarify: Force-fetching doesn't create any sort of retrieving instinct; your dog already possesses that. What it does is make your dog a 100-percent reliable retriever anytime, anywhere, no questions asked. There will come a time, whether it's tomorrow or next month or next year, when your dog will decide he would rather be doing something besides bringing you the bird you just sent him to pick up. If you have taken your dog through the force-fetching routine, he will do it anyway. If you haven't, well, I guess you can go pick up the bird yourself, which seems kind of silly if you're hunting with a "retriever."

Before you begin force-fetching, read this chapter thoroughly and ask yourself if you are committed to following it through to completion. This isn't something you do in a couple days, or even a couple weeks. It's a long, detailed process. So, if you have any doubts about whether you can do it, consider taking your dog to a reputable professional retriever trainer and hire him to take your dog through this process. On the other hand, if things have been going well so far and your dog understands the concept of pressure on, pressure off that has figured so prominently into many aspects of his training, you should certainly be able to do a good job on this.

1st SEMESTER HIGHLIGHTS

Getting Started

Adding a New Object

More Table Work

Finally, Down to the Ground

Training Dummies and Birds

Transition to Proper Delivery

Final Reinforcement

GETTING STARTED

As with Sit, Heel, Stay and other obedience commands, you don't ask your dog to do something; you tell him. So why would you ask him if he would like to retriever properly? You wouldn't.

Walk your dog back and forth on the table to get him comfortable moving around on it.

A dog that has completed his force-fetch training will reliably:

1. Hold an object on command for any amount of time you specify.
2. Pick an object up off the ground on command.
3. Deliver an object to your hand and not release it until you give a command.
4. Gently deliver birds to hand.

It's very important that you take care of all this prep work before trying to introduce new training concepts.

With those goals in mind, let's start by creating a work area. First, you need a sturdy table for your dog to stand on. It's much easier to work with him up at your level. Place the table against a wall and affix a short tether that keeps the dog secure so you are free to work with both hands.

Next, take some time to make sure your dog is comfortable being up on the table. You want him to accept the elevated position as something positive. Guide him on walks up and down the table so he gets comfortable moving around on it. It's very important that you take care of all this prep work before trying to introduce new training concepts.

Now, because force-fetching is all about the dog's mouth and because you are going to constantly be inserting and removing objects from his mouth, he has to be comfortable with that. Start the process with one hand inside a heavy leather glove. Insert your hand into the dog's mouth with your thumb under his jaw. Your dog isn't going to like this, and the first thing he's going to do is fight you. When this happens, don't give in. Tighten your grip as much as necessary, and don't let him win. This could go on for a few seconds or for quite a while. Either way, what you do next is key: The moment he stops fighting, say Drop while removing your hand. The goal of this drill, over a period of days, is for your dog to learn how to get rid of your hand. There is no verbal command for Hold with this drill, because it's not meant to teach him to hold something. That comes next, and you will find that if you start out with this gloved-hand drill, Hold is much easier to accomplish. Try to do this drill twice a day. Each session should comprise only four to five separate "hand in, hand out" sequences.

Some dogs catch on quicker than others, but they all eventually get it. After a number of sessions you will find that your dog doesn't fight the hand at all because he has learned that remaining still means the hand comes out. When you're getting no struggle you can introduce the Hold command. At this point, leave the hand in your dog's mouth a bit longer after the struggling ceases, saying Hold multiple times. Gradually increase the length of time you leave the hand in his mouth.

Your dog will need to be comfortable with you inserting and removing objects from his mouth.

This process is much better than using the word Hold in the early stages when he is fighting you. Do it that way and your dog associates Hold with stress. Take the time to introduce this as just described and you will be working with a much calmer dog that doesn't think Hold is something to fight about.

NEW PRESSURE

Next, you're going to come at this exercise from a different angle. Place your non-glove hand over the top of your dog's muzzle and press his jowls against his upper teeth until he opens his mouth. Insert the gloved hand and instantly remove the pressure from his jowls. After a few days of four to five sequences of this twice a day, you will see him start to open his mouth as soon as your hand comes over his muzzle. He is learning that he can avoid pressure by opening his mouth. Once you can tell he understands all of this, gradually extend the length of time you leave your hand in his mouth.

Now you are going to introduce yet another kind of pressure: the ear pinch. With your non-glove hand, grasp your dog's nylon collar in a way that you can reach his ear. If you are right-handed, your non-glove hand would be your left, so you are reaching over the top of the dog's neck and placing four fingers under the nylon collar, leaving your thumb free to grasp the ear. Pinch the ear by pressing it against the nylon collar with the side of your thumb or your thumbnail, whichever works best for you. At the same time, move your gloved hand toward his mouth.

Your dog will learn to turn off the pressure by opening his mouth.

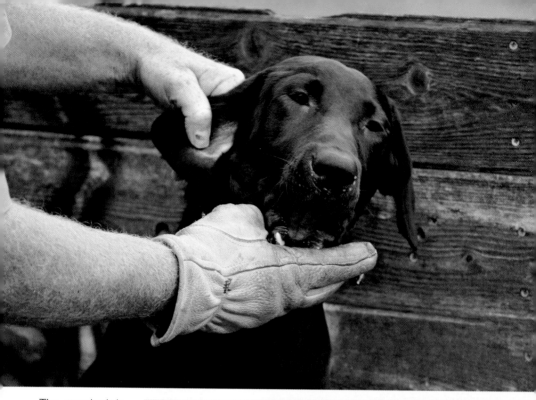

The ear pinch is another form of pressure which your dog learns to remove by opening his mouth.

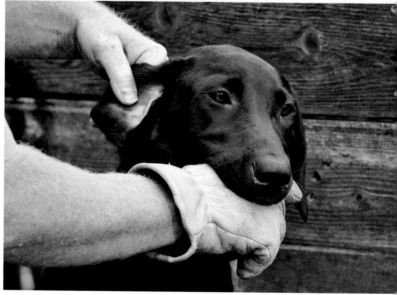

Some dogs require more of a pinch than others, but eventually they understand that this uncomfortable pinch is another form of pressure. And how does he remove the pressure? By opening his mouth. And what happens when he opens his mouth? You insert the gloved hand and stop pinching. Get it? Pressure on, pressure off. By this point your dog should get this concept as easily as you do.

If your dog doesn't seem to understand what you expect, go back: Do another couple sessions of delivering pressure via the jowl squeeze. In fact, there are few training problems that can't be solved by some retroactive drills. Each step in this book builds on the one before it. If a step is too challenging, drop back to whatever you were doing before. However, it is very important that if you take a step backwards, you must keep up the pressure – leash, choke chain, ear pinch, whatever – or your dog will get the idea that he has can avoid any new form or pressure by simply refusing a command. So, while it's okay to cut your dog some slack in how quickly he grasps a new concept, it is not okay to let him get away with it without consequences. Your dog must understand that the only way to avoid pressure is to comply.

When your dog understands that the sooner he opens his mouth, the sooner the ear pinch stops, he will actually start reaching for your hand as soon as it comes near his mouth, pressure or no pressure. This is exactly what you have been striving for. Now you know he really gets it. Every now and then, give him a "freebie" by not pinching his ear as he aggressively grabs for the object. This helps teach him he can avoid pressure by complying quickly.

At this stage, you can begin some proofing. Try this: See if you can sneak your hand out of his mouth. If he doesn't make some sort of attempt to keep holding on, immediately pinch his ear. He will quickly figure out that he needs to keep a firm grip on any object you tell him to hold. Now, if you try to slip your hand out and he firms up his grip, obviously you don't need to put any pressure on him. He is doing exactly what you want.

From this point forward, you can add a verbal Hold to the drill. Pretty simple really, and there will never be any confusion about what that word means.

ADDING A NEW OBJECT

Okay, the Hold concept is solid and, really, you've gotten through what is probably the toughest part of force-fetching. But you're still not done. Now you are going to introduce various objects, starting with a dowel stick. There are several commercial variations of this tool and it doesn't really matter which type you

use as long as it is of a configuration that is easy for your dog to pick up cleanly. Whatever type of dowel stick you work with, be sure to use it only for force-fetching drills.

Introduce the dowel stick via the ear pinch. All you're doing is trading your gloved hand for this new object. You should find that this transition goes pretty smoothly. If your dog puts up a fight or seems unsure about this new wrinkle, go back to the jowl pinch until he is complying. Then step up to the ear pinch. It should only take a few sessions, maybe a week, before your dog is reaching out to get the object – in essence he is trying to beat the pressure, and that's exactly what you want to see. Once he is really lunging for the dowel stick and holding it, try to sneak it out the way you did earlier with your gloved hand. How bad does he want to keep holding it? Pretty badly, I'll bet.

Don't be alarmed if you reach a point where it seems your dog absolutely doesn't want to let anything out of his mouth, even if you say Drop. Enforcing the "Drop" command is quite simple, and I will get to that shortly.

The next step is to make your dog work just a bit more to get ahold of the dowel stick. If he is reaching straight out a couple

Once your dog gets the glove drill, replace the gloved hand with a dowel stick.

inches to grab it with confidence, you can start moving the starting point down toward the table, a couple inches at a time. You can even move the stick down after he starts to reach, forcing him to really concentrate on your hand position and aggressively go after it.

This exercise teaches your dog to pick up an object from the table upon receiving the Fetch command.

Now it's time to add a verbal "Fetch" to the process. Your dog will quickly come to understand that he needs to get that object, any object, in his mouth right now, whether it's in your hand, on the ground or wherever. A bit of caution is in order here: Once you've introduced Fetch, don't use this word during fun retrieves. Likewise, refrain from using the word Hold at any time other than when you are working on force-fetching. Your dog has really felt some pressure over the past few weeks and that is his only point of reference for those words. So don't use them during fun time when he should be carefree and relaxed.

Finally, the pinnacle of this phase is that your dog will cleanly pick up an object off the tabletop upon receiving the Fetch command. When you get to this point you are truly in the home-stretch.

MORE TABLE WORK

Until now your dog has been in a stationary position during these drills. Now you are going to add yet another variation: Moving while still holding the dowel stick.

Start out with your dog holding the dowel stick and one hand underneath his collar. Now, simply start walking along the edge of the table, encouraging your dog to move along with you via Heel. This is new to him and he may want to drop the dowel when he

starts walking. If that happens, be ready to immediately apply the ear pinch and keep the pressure on while you pick up the up the dowel stick, hold it in front of him and command Fetch until the dowel stick is back in his mouth. If you're having trouble getting him to walk along with you while holding, simply stop wherever he's at and praise him while he holds the dowel stick. Be patient; he will get it. You will probably need a good week or so of this until your dog is reliably moving up and down the table while holding the dowel stick.

FINALLY, DOWN TO THE GROUND

You are about to find out just how reliable your dog is when it comes to Fetch and Hold. The first time you run through some table drills on the ground, how does it go? Will he snap the dowel stick off the ground every time or does he hesitate? Can you walk your dog at heel while he holds? If so, great. If he shows signs of weakness in certain aspects, well, at least you know what things you have to review back up on the table.

Whenever you introduce a variable to a known command or routine be prepared to do some retroactive training. It's about your dog's understanding and comfort level – and sometimes his sneaky efforts to simply get out of working. So be prepared for anything. The transition from the table to the ground is just one example. Once the ground work is going okay, take the drills to a new area of the yard or to a property your dog has never been. Expect issues to arise and be prepared to deal with them. Hopefully you have one of those easily adaptable, fast learners that takes these changes in stride. If not, as always, go back to what you were doing in the previous step until you're sure he gets it.

Another form of change is the introduction of different objects. Once things are going smoothly on the ground with the

Once the ground work is going okay, take the drills to a new area of the yard or to a property your dog has never been.

dowel stick, introduce a different object. I like to transition from the dowel stick to a canvas-covered stick or beanbag. Maybe he'll treat this new object no differently ... or maybe he'll balk at it. But if your force-fetch program has been consistent with no shortcuts there shouldn't be any huge issues. After that introduce another object. It shouldn't matter whether you're telling him to hold a plastic pop bottle, hammer handle or whatever. He

Once things are going smoothly with the dowel stick, introduce a different object.

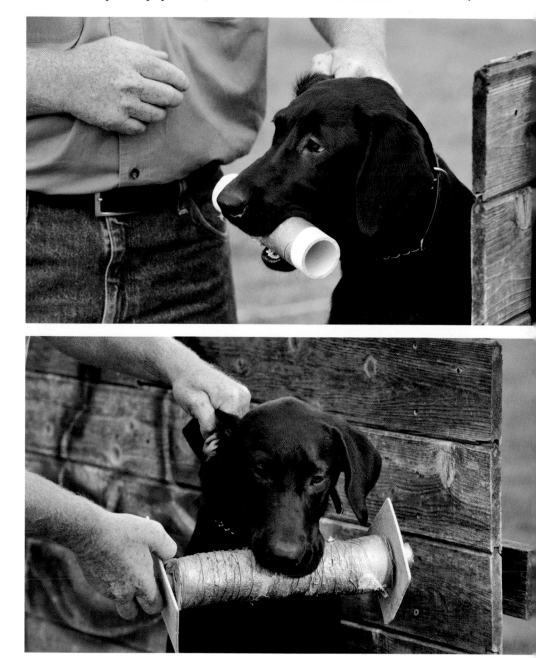

is supposed to know Fetch and Hold, and it's not your dog's job to decide what he'd like to pick up on any given day. As you use different objects, however, don't move on to a new one until he is perfectly compliant with the current one.

You'll notice I have not mentioned training dummies or birds yet. That comes next. First be sure your dog is 100 percent reliable with three or four other objects, meaning he will take them from your hand, pick them up from the ground and walk at heel without dropping them under any circumstances. If you have reached that point, you are now ready to reinforce the Drop command. With your dog sitting at your side and holding the dowel stick, reach for the stick while at the same time tightening the leash and stepping on your dog's near foot. You don't have to be aggressive about this; it doesn't take much pressure to cause him enough discomfort that he will open his mouth and release the object. This technique works so well that you have to make sure you don't overdo it and make your dog think that having something in his mouth is wrong. It should only take a couple sessions to make him understand. Hopefully after that you will only need to give an occasional reminder if he refuses to give up an object.

TRAINING DUMMIES AND BIRDS

Your dog loves retrieving the various bumpers and dummies you've been tossing for him, mostly in the context of a fun reward at the end of your training sessions. So now that he has made it through your force-fetching regimen, he finally gets to fetch and hold one of his favorite objects. Introduce it just like you did the last few objects, starting on the table and transitioning to the

When introducing a new variable, be prepared to take a step back and reinforce earlier lessons if necessary.

ground. Use some ear pinch pressure to start, but also give him a freebie now and then when he aggressively reaches for the bumper and scoops it right up. Praise like crazy when this happens. If you've made it this far I wouldn't anticipate any real problems with training dummies.

Next move on to a frozen pigeon. Again, this is something he knows and likes. Same routine as above. You might get a bit of mouthing or rolling the pigeon in his mouth initially but, again, if you've made it this far a bird shouldn't create any new problems.

TRANSITION TO PROPER DELIVERY

Now that your dog will reliably hold, you can begin insisting on a perfect delivery of any object to your hand from the heel position. This is called a good "finish" and it's another sign of a well-trained, in-control retriever.

Get out the platforms you used in earlier drills and have your dog sit on one while wearing his check cord. Have him hold the dowel stick while you walk to the other platform about six feet away. With the platform on your left (if you're a right-handed shooter who has trained your dog to heel on the left), call your dog

Use the platforms to teach your dog to deliver objects to your hand from the Heel position.

to you. He should go directly to the platform, swing around to the heel position and sit. Be ready with the check cord if he doesn't take a direct route to you or in some way won't go directly to the platform.

Command Drop and take the object from him. Give lots of praise, command Fetch and Hold, and walk back to the other platform. Repeat. When you are getting good compliance, move on to a new object. Work on this for a week or so, gradually moving increasing the platform distances to 30 feet or so. It won't be long before your dog knows you always expect him to finish his retrieves by coming to heel and sitting.

Always finish up these drills by tossing some fun bumpers. When you get to the point where you are doing finishing drills without the platforms while using his favorite dummy, you will be impressed by how anxious he is to charge back to you, spin 180 degrees and plant his rear next to you in anticipation of getting to run out for a fun retrieve. And that will be one of many times you will realize that the force-fetching routine was all worthwhile.

FINAL REINFORCEMENT

There is one more step to completing force-fetching, and that's reinforcement with the remote collar. You can't complete force-fetching without the remote collar, so I have included that portion at the end of the next chapter.

When you are getting good compliance, move on to a new object.

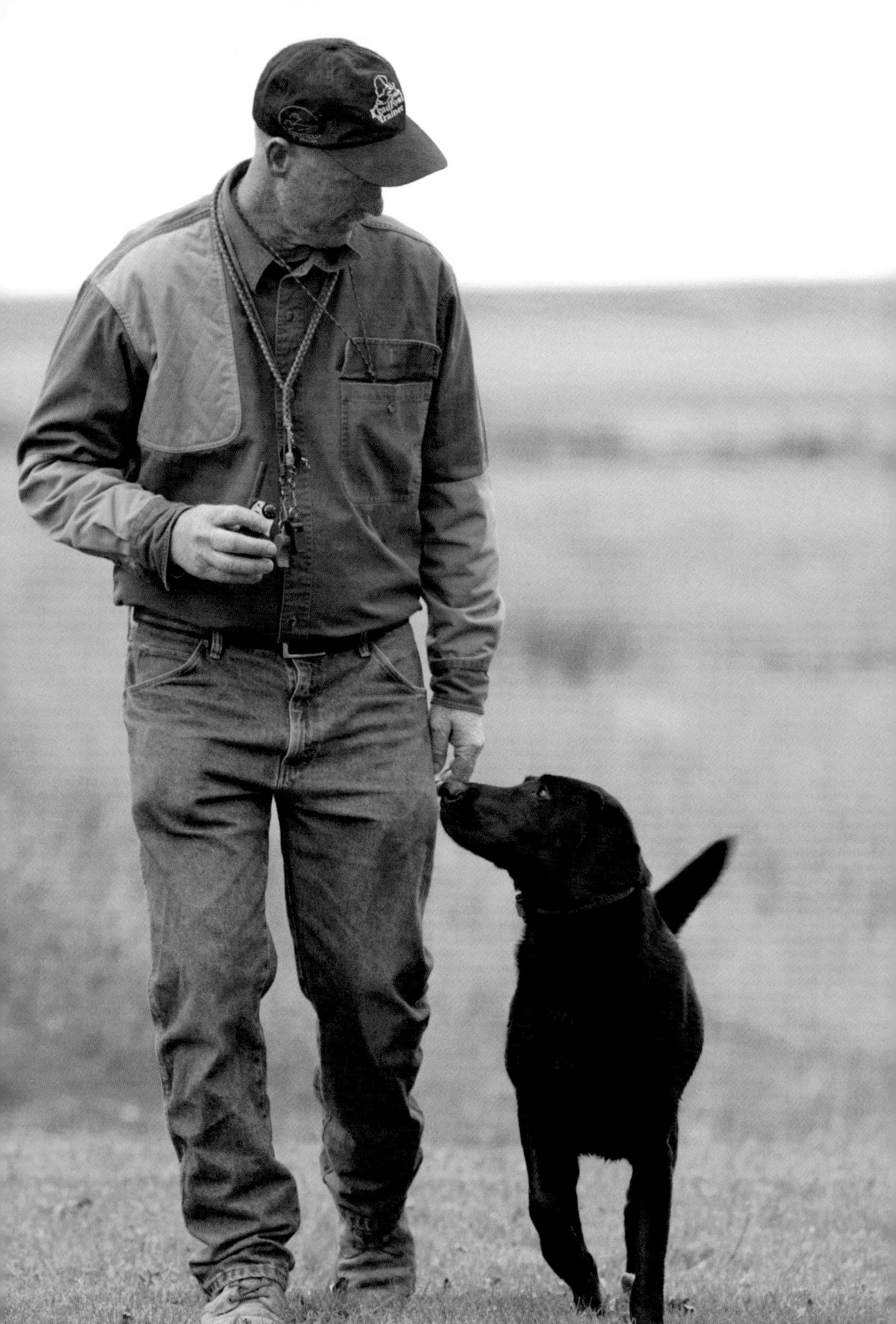

–10–
THE REMOTE COLLAR

**2nd
SEMESTER
HIGHLIGHTS**

Before You Start

Obedience...
One More Time

Nearing Off-Leash
Perfection

"Bulletproof"
Obedience

Important
Final Notes

Back To
Force-Fetching

Everyone has an opinion about the electronic, or "remote," collar. Let me suggest that the most important thing for you to know about it is this: Complete this chapter and you will have a dog that is truly obedient and in control at all times without the need for a leash or check cord. Pretty cool idea, isn't it? And the best part is, when you reach that goal, your dog is going to be as happy about it as you are!

The reason I'm confident that following these instructions will help you reach this point is that today you have available the finest training technology available in the form of a tool that has been evolving for close to 40 years. Today's remote collars help you reinforce commands you've already taught and can be used on dogs of virtually any size, breed, temperament or ability.

I have been presenting dog training seminars for 30 years, but only in the last several years have I incorporated the remote collar into my demonstrations. That's because until recently the remote collar was only meant for one type of dog: The stubborn one that was only reliable if he was being coerced by high-level electronic stimulation. Older remote collars had one setting: Hot!

Now everything's changed. Today's collars offer multiple levels that begin with a barely perceptible tickle. You have the ability to adapt the collar to your dog, not the other way around. The collar delivers an electronic stimulation, or stimulus. If you've never felt it, I can best describe it as static electricity. Many dogs can't even feel the lowest levels. In fact, on most of today's remote collars, if you touch the contact points while I press a transmitter button that delivered the lowest-level stimulus you would likely think that the collar wasn't work-

HIGH SCHOOL – 8 TO 9 MONTHS

ing because you wouldn't feel anything. The pressure you deliver with a choke chain is more intense than a low-level remote collar correction.

So, which level will your dog respond to? We'll get to that in a second. First I need to point out that at the other end of the spectrum, the high stimulation levels are still available. But modern training techniques for the most part don't require their use. These are better kept in reserve for emergencies such as if your dog takes off chasing a deer or runs toward a busy highway and you need to stop him immediately.

BEFORE YOU START

You need to take care of some things before you ever even think about turning on the remote collar. As noted in earlier chapters, you have to get your dog used to wearing it. It's very important that he associates the collar with fun and freedom. Whether you're just letting him out to run in the yard, taking him for a walk or throwing fun bumpers, if he's feeling that familiar weight of the remote collar while he's having fun, he won't associate the collar with corrections. You don't want your dog to think that the only time he has to listen is when he's wearing it.

I shouldn't have to also tell you, but I will anyway, that your dog needs to be perfect on his obedience commands before you can start remote collar training. If he knows his obedience, then you did a good job of teaching him the concept of pressure on, pressure off. And if he knows how to turn off pressure from the choke chain, leash and check cord, it won't take much effort for him to figure out how to turn off remote collar pressure.

OBEDIENCE … ONE MORE TIME

You have taught your dog several obedience commands. That was the hard part. Now, you are going to simply run through them again while introducing the final type of pressure that your dog must understand if you want him to perform with absolute reliability off-leash. In all of these exercises, you are using constant or "continuous" remote collar stimulus. Deliver the stimulus upon giving the verbal command, and leave the stimulus on until the dog has completed the command.

These exercises require that you understand the collar and transmitter functions perfectly. It is important that you always use the lowest stimulus level necessary to get the required action from your dog, and that you always stop the stimulus the second he complies. I'm going to run through each command one more time so it's perfectly clear how everything fits together. With each

The moment your dog complies with the Heel command, release the button.

of these commands, start out using the leash or check cord and choke chain in tandem with the remote collar. Your dog already responds to pressure from the choke chain; he will accept that the remote collar stimulus is just an extension of that pressure. Once he makes the connection, it's quite easy to transition to pressure from the remote collar alone.

Start the introduction to the remote collar with a movement command. The reason for this is simple: If you start out teaching a

command such as Sit, your dog learns that if he remains stationary he avoids pressure. That would be fine if all you wanted your dog to do was sit, but it would make other commands more difficult to teach. Also, the commands you're about to review again aren't supposed to take place during some 45-minute training marathon. Just the opposite: do short lessons of just a few minutes at a time, two or three times a day, and always end up with something fun. On that note, let's start with Heel.

Continue with heeling exercises, and add a remote collar stimulus with the Sit command.

Heel – With your dog sitting next to you, command Heel and give a tug on the leash along with a tap of the transmitter's continuous button. As soon as he complies with the command release the button. You're teaching him that moving with you is the way to avoid pressure. Do this lesson two to three times a day for a few days. When you stop, command Sit, reinforcing with leash pressure if necessary. You will add the remote collar to the Sit command in the next step.

Note: Before going any further, I emphasize again that you should be using the lowest level of stimulus necessary to get a response. If your dog doesn't seem to be feeling the stimulus – as indicated by twitching his ear, blinking or cocking his head – you might have to move up a level. You aren't trying to get a big reaction from your dog, and you certainly don't want him to vocalize. It takes some time to learn how much remote collar pressure your dog needs. Also keep in mind that different situations may require higher correction levels. When your dog is excited or his attention is diverted, you maybe have to go up a level or two to get him to comply.

Sit – When your dog is responding quickly and positively to Heel, you have accomplished teaching him that all-important concept of responding to pressure by moving. Now you have to teach him that pressure can also mean Stop. Continue with your

heeling exercises, but now add a remote collar stimulus with the word Sit. As soon as his rear hits the ground, release the button and leash pressure.

Note: As I've mentioned before, when your dog is responding well to pressure of any type as you go through various drills, it is okay to give him that "freebie" every now and then. For example, after responding to Sit and low-level stimulus three times in a row, don't use the remote collar on the fourth one. This helps develop a quick response to a command because he's learning that instant compliance may help him avoid pressure.

Place/Kennel – Your dog should obviously have a complete understanding of both Place and Kennel, which are really the same command with different destinations. Now you're simply going to reinforce these commands with the remote collar. Set that familiar platform out in the yard and work on heeling exercises. With your dog walking at heel, head toward the platform and then, from about six feet away, command Place while applying continuous stimulus with the remote collar. Continue walking with him right up to the platform. As always, as soon as he is up on the platform, release the button. Now, if your dog steps off the platform before you have given him an Okay or some other release command, you must be quick on the continuous button

When introducing the remote collar, remember to continue using leash pressure to guide your dog.

and keep pressing it until you have guided him back up onto the platform with leash pressure at the same time. Again, your dog just learned how to turn off this new form of pressure. Reinforcing Kennel looks the same as Place, you simply use his travel kennel instead of the platform.

Come – If your dog has a complete understanding of his commands, reinforcing Come with the remote collar should not be difficult. Keep in mind that you just finished teaching him that leav-

ing the platform after being given the Place command is wrong, so it's very important that you can control and guide him with the leash for this command. You would not want your dog to freeze in place because he feels safe on the platform. With your dog on the platform, step back about six feet and command Come while applying a continuous remote collar stimulus and leash pressure. Keep the stimulus on until your dog gets all the way to your side. Remember, lots of praise!

When using the collar to teach Come, keep the stimulus on until your dog gets all the way to your side.

Once he's got it using platforms, move to another area and give Come command using leash and remote collar.

Down – This is one command that requires a different remote collar position. Before you work on Down, put the collar on your dog with the contact points on the back of his neck instead of underneath. This really helps a dog understand the command. In the past, pressure on Down came from you pushing down on his neck. Well, now there's still pressure in the same place; it's just coming from a different source. As with the other commands, use pressure from the leash in tandem with the continuous button until your dog is all the way down to the ground, then release the pressure. If he gets up or moves before you release him, be ready to apply pressure again, and keep it on until he is back into the down position.

NEARING OFF-LEASH PERFECTION

How long should it take to reinforce all of these commands with the remote collar? Well, two weeks is a pretty good goal if you keep in mind that, once your dog understands the concept, you need to repeat the drills and then repeat them some more. If you need longer than that, no problem. Also, if you sense that your dog really doesn't understand a certain command, you have no business introducing the remote collar. Go back and do some retroac-

tive leash training until you know that he gets it. Remember, the remote collar is not a shortcut, it is a reinforcement tool that makes your finished product better.

The next step is to work on all of these commands with no leash pressure at all. Leave the leash attached to the dog's choke chain as a backup measure if you need it, but if you have done a thorough teaching job you should rarely have to reach for it.

This first portion of "obedience proofing" should take place in a confined area such as a fenced backyard. It should also be free of distractions – startling noises, kids, other dogs, etc. This is a time when you really have to concentrate and honestly assess whether your dog truly "gets" each command, or if he has only been achieving success when you are guiding him or correcting his mistakes.

Run through each command over a period of a few days. Then link commands together, two or three at a time. Remember, the leash is always there if you need it, but hopefully your dog is quickly responding to your voice commands and reinforcement from the collar when necessary. If your dog ever seems confused or hesitant, take a step back and teach the command again with leash pressure. As you should understand by now, the progression of this book is such that you always have that option. This has been true from the

Once your dog performs all commands with the remote collar dragging the leash, review all commands without the leash.

earliest chapters when you were teaching your pup the most basic concepts. Every lesson builds upon the one before it.

So take several days to work on these commands, all the while honestly assessing your dog's understanding and, really, how good a job you have done in helping him understand what you expect from him.

"BULLETPROOF" OBEDIENCE

It's one thing for your dog to perform commands in simple situations without distractions. It is quite another for him to be perfectly obedient when there are several things vying for his attention. So it's very important that you run through these obedience drills in less-than-ideal situations. After all, there will be times – actually, most of the time – in the field when multiple and sometimes unplanned circumstances influence his performance.

For example, you're in a duck blind. Your buddy is blowing a duck call, a dozen mallards are circling your decoys, a flock of coots is swimming by just 20 yards away, someone in the distance

fires a gun, a dog on the other side of the river is barking … Are you confident your dog understands that Place means stay put until you tell him differently?

Distractions occur in upland hunting as well. Some guys across the road are shooting at a pheasant, your hunting partner is blowing his whistle while trying to control his own dog, a rooster flushes wild 100 yards down the field and your dog just saw a rabbit go streaking into a brushpile … Does your dog understand that Come means he needs to get over to you right now, not only when he feels like it?

Now, I know you thought you were done with the choke chain and leash after the last section, but you need to pick up these tools one more time. You will need them for backup reinforcement during some exercises in which you are going to purposely create distractions.

Start out in the backyard with your dog comfortably heeling on a loose leash. Walk back and forth past a friend or family member, each time passing by a bit closer. If your dog wants to dart over to that person and start playing because he thinks that would be

more fun than walking around with you, command Heel and give a tug on the leash while applying continuous remote collar stimulus. Your dog might make the mistake of leaving your side a couple times but, after you correct him, he should figure our pretty quickly that it's just easier and less stressful to follow your directions.

Earlier I mentioned that there will be times when your dog requires a higher stimulus level if you are to get him back under control. This is one of those times. When your dog gets excited and distracted he can easily ignore a stimulus level that would normally get his attention in a more controlled situation. Again, just be aware of this and make sure you have a complete understanding of your remote collar and transmitter functions so you can properly increase the stimulus level without overdoing it. In time you will gain a very clear understanding of how much pressure your dog requires in various situations.

Once you have made the point that it is unacceptable for your dog to run around and greet every person he sees, repeat the drill, this time with your helper in a crouched position. Your dog will probably regard this body language as someone who wants to play with him. Again, heel your dog back and forth several times, each time passing by a little closer, the last time coming within six or eight feet. This is just a basic distraction. Don't have your helper clap or talk; at this point just having another person in the yard is enough of a temptation.

Where you go with this process from here is largely dependent on how easily you are able to steer your dog away from distractions. You can do your heeling drill with additional people in the yard. You can have friend bring his leashed dog into the yard as a new temptation. Don't be surprised if each time you ramp up the distraction level your dog wants to check it out. Calmly and consistently use as much correction as is necessary to show your dog that doing anything other than what you want is unacceptable. After awhile, your dog is going to figure out that you've been setting him up, and he will look at any type of distraction in a different light.

After a week or so of distraction training, get rid of the leash and try him again, relying solely on the remote collar to make corrections when necessary. Make distractions complex, because they certainly are in the real world. In time, your dog will focus on the task at hand and nothing else, and you can be proud of a job well done.

IMPORTANT FINAL NOTES

Here are a few items to keep in mind as you work toward completing off-leash training:

1. If you are the type of person with a short fuse, keep that temper under control when training with the remote collar. Pushing a transmitter button is easy, but that doesn't mean you need to do it a lot. Remember, the remote collar is about reinforcing, not punishing.

2. As you work on obedience commands, keep in mind the power of their meanings and avoid using them during fun time. For example, let's say you spent a lot of time working on the Come command and maybe you had to apply a good amount of pressure to get your dog to comply consistently. Then the lesson ends and you toss a fun bumper. Just as your dog picks it up, you holler Come! Your dog thinks, "Yikes! I guess fun time is over. I'd better drop this dummy and get back over there!" So be aware of the meaning that these words take on and be smart about how you use them. Make sure fun time remains fun.

BACK TO FORCE-FETCHING

The end of the last chapter mentioned that the final step in force-fetch training is to reinforce it with the remote collar. You were using pressure in the form of an ear pinch. Now, for the final

When combining the collar and ear pinch, your dog will quickly grab the stick, just as he did to turn off ear pressure alone.

step in force-fetch training, you will go through the drills again, incorporating remote collar stimulus as well.

The "beginning of the end" of finishing force-fetching takes place with your dog back up on the table. Get your fetching stick, which was the first object you taught your dog to hold on the table, and hold it out a few inches from his mouth. Apply ear pressure and continuous low-level collar stimulus at the same time. It's very important to use the lowest stimulus your dog can feel, which may be a level or two below the one you finished obedience proofing with. What you should expect is that your dog will quickly grab the stick just like he did after he figured out how to turn off ear pressure.

After a couple successful sessions, gradually work the stick down closer to the table. Depending on how smoothly things progress, you should have him picking the stick up off the table within several sessions. If at any point your dog balks or seems to lack confidence, back up a step and make sure he understands what you expect of him before moving forward.

Next, start the drill all over again, but without the ear pinch. Work the starting point down closer to the table with each session, just like you did in the last chapter. When he's reliably snapping up the stick from the table, follow up with some walking up and down the table carrying it. All good? Okay, now it's down to the ground. Same set of drills, just in a different environment: Ear pinch and remote collar together, followed by remote collar pressure only.

When you have perfect compliance it's time to introduce a new object. Your routine is the same one you followed in the last chapter except you start with dual pressure instead of the ear pinch alone. Most importantly, don't take shortcuts. When you change objects, it's back up to the table to start. And I can't say it enough: If your dog hesitates at any stage, go back one step until he's fully compliant before moving forward again.

Congratulations again! You've made it through all the basics of force-fetching reinforcement with the remote collar. Now it's time

If your dog seems to lack confidence, back up a step and make sure he knows what you expect of him.

Once your dog is reliably snapping up the stick from the table, have him walk back and forth on the table carrying the stick.

An excellent proofing exercise for this is the walk-up drill.

to complete your force-fetching drills off-leash at ground level. An excellent proofing exercise for this is the walk-up drill. While walking your dog at heel, drop the fetching stick behind you and then keep on walking. After six or seven more steps, turn and come back toward the stick. As you get close to it, command Fetch but do not stop walking. After he picks it up, continue walking with him at heel carrying the object. Stop, have him sit and then take then take it from him. Repeat with different objects, the goal of course being that your dog grabs any object, any time, on command with no pressure.

If you were pleased with your dog's response to force-fetching at the end of the last chapter, you will be amazed at how much sharper he is after you've gone through this final phase using remote collar reinforcement.

–11–
ADVANCED RETRIEVING

When you think about it, almost everything we have covered to this point somehow ties into making your dog a more reliable retriever. You finished his off-leash obedience, so you should have no issues with him performing at long distances. And you completed his force-fetch training, so there shouldn't be any problems with picking up, carrying and holding birds. Also, as part of his force-fetch training, you taught your dog to properly present the bird to you in a well-executed finish. All of these parts come together now as you work on strengthening his retrieving abilities.

Just as important as the act of running out, picking up a bird and bringing it back is the ability to remain steady and not go anywhere until you want him to. While it is exciting to see your dog run long distances to pick up birds, you will never get there if he isn't calmly watching the fall with his rear planted at heel. So let's review some steadiness issues before we get to the retrieving portion of this chapter.

**LAST MONTH
SENIOR YEAR
HIGHLIGHTS**

True Steadiness

Introducing
Long Retrieves

Water Work

Adding Difficulty

Doubling Up

Let's Go
Hunting!

TRUE STEADINESS

Your dog knows Place and Stay. You have tempted him to leave his platform and corrected him when he did so. At this point he should have absolutely no issues with staying put until you allow him to move. This is an area that people too frequently gloss over in their eagerness to do the much more exciting retrieving drills. But that's a mistake. A dog that is fidgety while sitting at heel isn't concentrating on "marking," or seeing the dummy or bird fall. He needs to be composed and focused, not thinking about how to get away with creeping out of position.

Sometimes a dog will outright "break" to go after a retrieve before his handler releases him. This is a car-

HIGH SCHOOL – 9 MONTHS TO 1 YEAR

dinal sin, and you can't tolerate it. Because you took the time to properly do the platform work, if you do have to make a correction for breaking your dog will understand he's being busted for ignoring an obedience command and not because he wants to retrieve.

At this stage you are nearly finished with the platform forever. Soon, anyplace you command your dog to sit and stay will be the platform. This is true whether he is sitting at heel, at the front of your boat or in the corner of the duck blind. Before you start the drills in the next section, make sure your dog understands that.

With your dog on the platform, do a bit of proofing by walking circles around him while swinging a dummy. If he steps off,

At this point, your dog should stay put until you allow him to leave the platform.

deliver a continuous stimulus with the remote collar and keep it on until he is back on the platform. Next, wander out about 10 yards and pop the blank pistol a few times. Again, if he leaves deliver a continuous correction until he's back to his spot. Be aware that his excitement level might be pretty high because of his love for gunshots, so you might have to bump up the correction level. It shouldn't take more than a few shots for him to get the message.

Every now and then after your dog has resisted temptation, give him an Okay, letting him know he's free to move around.

Next, take a long stick and tether a live pigeon to it by attaching a two-foot length of decoy line to the bird's leg. The pigeon will be able to flutter but can't get away. Stand several yards in front of your dog with the pigeon on the ground. Let it walk around, and then lift up on the stick to try to get it to flutter. Make sure you are

always ready to quickly lift the bird up and away from the dog if he should try to grab it. At the same time you have to be quick on the continuous button and instantly tell your dog Place if he comes off the platform. Again, after a successful session of resisting temptation, be sure to give him the Okay.

Lastly, put your dog's choke chain on again and attach a leash while he's also wearing his remote collar. Have a helper stand out in front at about 30 yards and swing a dummy around, trying to excite your dog. If your dog stays put, have him toss the dummy. If your dog breaks, give him a stout correction with both the leash and remote collar. But if he doesn't break, great! Release him for the short retrieve by simply saying his name. He won't know that this means he can leave, so you will probably have to use his name in tandem with Okay. It won't be long before he understands that his name is your retrieve command.

If your dog breaks, quickly lift away the bird, give the Place command, and apply the collar stimulus.

Progress through
these exercises
until you are do-
ing the shooting,
using a shotgun.

When you first bring a thrower into this drill it's also time to introduce the word "Mark." This is simply your dog's cue to concentrate on what's going on out in front of him. In the next section, when you start actual retrieving drills, always give your dog a Mark so he is looking for the source of the retrieve you're about to send him on.

After a couple days of this, have your thrower pop the blank gun before throwing, adding another element of excitement. (Keep these throws short – 30 yards max. Remember, this is a steadiness drill, not a retrieving exercise.) Always be ready for your dog to make a mistake. In fact, expect it. You're putting all his favorite stuff out there in front of him and he wants it! Now, even though you are ready to make a correction with the remote collar if your dog breaks, make sure your thrower knows that it's his job to hustle after the dummy and pick it up before your dog gets to it. This is very important. Your dog must never be rewarded for breaking. If he gets to that dummy just one time, he may very well continually test you in hopes of getting it again by breaking.

Next, do the shooting yourself. After all, that's how it will be in the real world. No breaking? Great. Send him for the retrieve. If all goes well, graduate to where you're shooting a shotgun. And, finally, comes the ultimate steadiness proofing. Get a second helper to throw a live bird and have the other helper shoot it. Now it's all there: flapping wings, a shotgun blast and a real bird tumbling to earth in plain sight while your dog trembles with excitement. Does he stay put? Yes? That's success! Awesome and congratulations – you can finally get rid of the platform!

Every now and then, when your dog has resisted temptation, remember to reward him.

Now what? Well, it's pretty simple: Run through the program again with no platform. Keep the leash handy for extra reinforcement in the early stages of this, but hopefully your transition from platform steadiness to just plain steadiness will not be terribly difficult. Expect your dog to test you a bit at first. Of course, if your dog breaks at this point you can't say Place because there is no more identifiable "place." Instead, in the event of breaking, you say No and Heel while applying leash and/or continuous collar pressure to bring him back to your side.

INTRODUCING LONG RETRIEVES

One huge part of developing a well-rounded retriever is making sure he can complete long-distance retrieves. Therefore, a reliable helper who can throw dummies and birds for you is a must. A second component in this equation is a wide-open field with little or no cover. Getting a dog to run far and straight has everything to do with vision; this isn't supposed to be about searching with his nose. Here's what the program looks like:

Your dog is sitting at heel. Your helper has a handful of dummies or birds and is standing in plain sight 20 yards away. He hollers or shoots to get your dog's attention and tosses the object. Because your dog has been trained to not move until you tell him, he remains seated next to you. After the object lands you say your dog's name, which is his cue to retrieve. While he's running out to make the retrieve, you backpedal 20 yards. Your dog returns with the dummy and delivers it to you. Now the distance between you and the thrower is 40 yards. Repeat. Now you're 60 yards apart. Repeat. Now you're 80 or so yards apart. Repeat.

There you go – you have dog doing nearly football-field length retrieves. Awesome! Except you're nowhere near finished. You can't assume that when you come back to this same place tomorrow you will be able to set up an 80-yard retrieve and your dog will perform flawlessly. As with everything else you've done, you have to work in small steps. So, on day two of this drill, start at 50 yards – tougher than 20, not as demanding as 80. Progress as above. Within a couple days you will be stretching things out to the 120-yard mark.

I would be remiss if I didn't mention another tool you can use when a helper isn't available: the handheld dummy launcher. After all, you might not always be able to find a thrower to help you train, but you don't want to miss out on training opportunities because of it. That's where the launcher comes in. This handy device, which is powered by a .22 blank cartridge, can fire a bumper anywhere from 40 yards to well beyond 100 yards, depending on the strength of the cartridge, wind direction and the angle you hold it when firing. I have to caution you not to start flinging dummies at distances your dog isn't ready for. Be

Use the launcher
when necessary,
but be sure to
keep shots within
distances that
ensure success.

sure to practice with the launcher and learn how far different types of bumpers will fly when using different-strength charges. It's very tempting to start firing at long distances just because you can … but if the result is that your dog hunts short, that's a setback. So, use the launcher when necessary, but make sure you keep the shots within distances that ensure success.

Let your dog dictate the pace. Build upon success, but take retroactive measures if necessary. If your dog shows signs of waning interest before you've reached your distance goal for the day, stop. Remember earlier when I said you always want to leave him wanting one more retrieve? Your dog is older now, but that still applies. If he ever seems hesitant to run the whole distance, either because he seems worried about getting too far from you or because he isn't confident that he's running right to the object, shorten the distance and build it back up from there.

Now, if you have a dog that is all fired up about retrieving but stops short and starts hunting because for some reason he doesn't see the bird lying where your helper threw it, have your assistant holler or shoot and toss another mark that lands right where the first one did.

A reasonable goal would be for your dog to be capable of 200-yard retrieves. Repeat, repeat, repeat the above sessions. As long as you are able to finish on a successful note, start the next session about 30 yards or so short of the previous day's maximum. It's not unreasonable to expect that you'll be able to reach the 200-yard mark within a week's time.

WATER WORK

It's more difficult to constantly change distances when setting up water retrieves. That's why I started this chapter with all land work. It's much easier to work on long-distance water retrieves when you have built up your dog's confidence on land. You already know your dog can make 30- to 40-yard water retrieves because that's how far you've been able to throw a dummy. A good goal for water work is for your dog to be able to complete 150-yard retrieves. Therefore you need a body of water at least that wide.

Just as you did on land, start with simple, close retrieves. Have your dog sit at heel just a few feet from shore. Your thrower, meanwhile, is in a boat about 50 yards out on the pond. The rate at which you increase the distance will depend on how confident of a swimmer your dog is. As on land, if the dog stops short of the mark and starts swimming around in circles like he's looking for the dummy, have your helper, holler or shoot and throw another dummy. (By the way, another nice touch during water retrieving sessions is for your helper to blow a duck call to get your dog's attention – it just adds

Helping your dog learn to hunt in cover during water retrieves takes a bit more logistical planning on your part.

some more realism to the drill and, hopefully, gets your dog even more excited.)

Increase the water retrieves 20 yards at a time. Obviously your helper has to do the moving. He should be able to easily relocate to his next position while your dog is swimming back to you with the dummy. As on land, start each new day's session about 20 yards closer than the maximum retrieve from the day before, and then work out from there.

ADDING DIFFICULTY

Because your dog will rarely have the luxury of taking a line to a bird that is lying in plain sight in actual hunting situations, you have to add some difficulty to these marking drills, both on land and in the water. On land, simply find a field with enough cover – perhaps a foot high – so that your dog will have to use his nose when he gets near the area of the fall. This is a great experience- and confidence-builder. Over time he will get better at marking the bird down and accurately gauging the distance to it. He will also learn to get downwind of the fall and use his nose to move in those last several yards and find the bird.

It's not unusual for a dog to hunt short of the fall in cover. Make sure your helper understands it's his job to be ready to throw another dummy if your dog slows down or starts hunting before getting to the area of the fall.

Helping your dog learn to hunt in cover during water retrieves takes a bit more logistical planning on your part. You can't expect your dog to willingly plunge into a six-foot high tangle of cattails the first time your helper tosses a dummy into that mess. If you can find a pond or the bay of a lake with some light marsh grass growing in the water, that would be ideal. In any event, the whole point is that you want your dog to eagerly search thick cover for downed ducks, and the only way to get him to do that is to practice. Otherwise you might end up with a dog that will only do water retrieves when a bird falls on the flat, calm surface of open water. You know that is often not the case, so teach him to aggressively search cover.

DOUBLING UP

Every now and then you and a hunting buddy will drop two birds at once, so it's nice if your dog understands that you have a preferred, systematic way of handling a double retrieve. I introduce the concept in the yard by having my dog sit at heel while I hold two dummies. These dummies should be white or at least very light-colored so your dog has no problem seeing them standing out against the short grass. It's very important he can pick

As with the other exercises, gradually increase distance, and progress from blank gun to shotgun.

them out at a glance, because this is the first time you're going to send him to retrieve something that he had to take his eyes off of before going after it.

Although your dog is obedient off-leash, you will want to have a leash attached to his choke chain for this drill. The reason for this is that you are going to toss one dummy, and then turn to toss the other one. Understandably, your dog will not want to turn away from the first dummy. After all, you've been running nothing but single retrieves his whole life. A leash will simply help you swing him around in the other direction if he won't turn when you do.

So line up and toss one dummy. Turn 180 degrees while commanding Heel and toss the other one. Send him for the second toss. As your dog returns to you, turn and face the first dummy and send him for that one.

Work on this daily and, as your dog becomes comfortable with the system, gradually narrow the angle between the tosses down to 90 degrees. If things are going well, go back out to that open field where you introduced long retrieves and use two throwers to toss short retrieves. The first time you run doubles with throwers have them stand at the 180-degree positions, working them toward 90 degrees over a period of days.

As that angle between the two throws narrows some dogs become tempted to run for one dummy, pick it up and then run over to the other one. Simply be aware that this could happen. The proper response from you is No! and Come! if you see him running in any direction except back to you after picking up the first mark. Also, make sure both throwers are aware that this situation could develop and that they know enough to run out and pick up the dummy if they see the situation deteriorating.

Part of what goes into developing a good doubles dog is developing his memory. After all, he has to watch two objects fall, put all his concentration into retrieving one of them and then go back for the other. An excellent drill that helps your dog become a strong marker is to have your helper throw some 70-yard singles, all at the same spot in very light cover. After your dog has run that same line a few times, have your helper throw it again, but this time, turn 90 degrees and toss a short retrieve yourself. Send your dog for the mark you tossed and then send him for the longer bird. Over time you can decrease the number of throws from your helper, forcing your dog to rely more on his memory rather than repetition.

Doubles drills are really only limited to your imagination. Have fun with it. At this point you have a rock-solid, steady retriever, so go ahead and build in some challenges. But don't set him up to fail; set him up for big success by building on the small successes.

At this point you have a rock-solid, steady retriever, so go ahead and build in some challenges.

LET'S GO HUNTING!

So much of what you've read about thus far has to do with simulating hunting, it's hard to believe you're actually going to get to the field someday with a totally reliable, fully trained retriever. But if you've completed this chapter, you're there!

The next chapter covers some of the realities you and your dog will face out in the real world. But remember that even though you're finally out of the early learning stages and heading into the big leagues you should never be hesitant to drop back and review any of the material you've already been through. If you're on the proposed timetable laid out at the beginning of each chapter, your dog isn't even a year old yet so perfection isn't a realistic goal. Even if it's the middle of hunting season, if problems crop up take the time to fix them through retroactive training. You and your retriever have many hunting seasons ahead of you. Spending a bit of extra time now to do things correctly will pay dividends for years to come.

–12–

REAL-WORLD CONSIDERATIONS

When you think about it, almost everything we have covered to this point somehow ties into making your dog a more reliable retriever. You finished his off-leash obedience, so you should have no issues with him performing at long distances. And you completed his force-fetch training, so there shouldn't be any problems with picking up, carrying and holding birds. Also, as part of his force-fetch training, you taught your dog to properly present the bird to you in a well-executed finish. All of these parts come together now as you work on strengthening his retrieving abilities.

Previous chapters offered tips and drills to get your dog ready for hunting in the real world. These comments revolved around things you can do to ensure success on early outings (i.e. by go to a game farm) and make your dog a more effective hunter (i.e. plant birds and encourage him to hunt the best cover). Now, with a fully or near-fully developed retriever, you are eager to get him out to go after wild birds. There will be times – actually, more often than not – when you can't control situations as tightly as you would like. You can't dictate when the ducks will work your decoys or whether a field will be full of pheasants, but you can be prepared for the inevitable surprises, annoyances, difficulties and emergencies that crop up in the world of hunting.

It just makes sense to be prepared, so let's run through some common scenarios and how to deal with them. Hopefully your outings will be more enjoyable and productive.

WATERFOWL CONSIDERATIONS

Whether you hunt ducks and geese from a boat, the shoreline or in a field, it is imperative that you always consider your dog's vision. For example, you can't expect him to be successful if you shove him to the

LAST MONTH SENIOR YEAR HIGHLIGHTS

Waterfowl Considerations

Upland Hunting

The Party Hunting Factor

Stuff You Need

Travel Notes

back of a blind with four-foot walls and then shoot ducks that he can't see fall. One way or another you have to set up so he can see well. Also, most waterfowl trips begin in the pre-dawn darkness. This is something new to your dog so cut him some slack if he seems apprehensive or fidgety.

No matter how many Stay drills you've done, you can't expect your young dog to be perfectly behaved for hours on end. His attention span at this stage simply won't allow it. I suggest your first real waterfowl hunt be no more than an hour or hour and half. Do your best to pick a time and place where you're almost guaranteed success. You wouldn't take a 10-year-old child on a six-hour muskie-fishing trip; no, you'd go to the pond where you knew he could catch lots of bluegills in a short period of time. Same idea with your dog. And don't hesitate to bring the leash along. You might be glad you have it handy if you need to show him that the game may have changed a bit the rules are still the same.

By the way, as basic as this sounds, please make sure that when ducks do finally come in somebody shoots them. With all the excitement of duck calls quacking and shotguns blasting, it would be nice if your dog gets some action! You might even be best served by letting a buddy or two do all the shooting the first few times out. That way you can give your full attention to your newest hunting partner. The first season should be all about him. If it involves more retriever training than serious hunting, so be it.

Another tip: If your dog isn't capable of doing blind retrieves, take along a bunch of golfball-sized rocks and keep them handy. If

you drop a bird that your dog didn't see fall, or if he needs something to focus on if he gets off-track while swimming, a well-placed splash or two near the duck will help him be successful.

Lastly, always take along his favorite dummy and loosen him up with some retrieves if the action is slow. That way, even if the ducks aren't cooperating on a particular day, your dog goes home having had a fun, positive experience.

UPLAND HUNTING

I can't stress enough how helpful game farms are in the early stages of upland training. If you have a bad outing or two on wild birds and it seems like your dog's interest is waning, take a trip to a game farm and work on the issues.

When a dog isn't finding birds and starts to lose motivation the first thing he'll do is start plodding. Next, if he gets really bored or tired or both, he'll walk behind you. If this happens you can discourage him by bumping him under the chin with your heels. Of course, a smart dog will simply move further back to avoid that unpleasantness and you'll be left to bust the cover yourself while your retriever ambles along behind you. The best solution is to simply never let it get to that point. Target times and places where you will have a high probability of getting into birds and use the game farm as your backup option.

An inevitable part of upland hunting is the bird that flies off without getting shot. It could be a rooster that gets up out of range, a hen that you don't shoot at or a bird that you shoot at but miss. Naturally your dog will want to give chase. At that moment you have a decision to make. You can try to call him back even though he's running off at warp speed, or you can let him chase and learn pretty quickly that there's no way he can ever catch a hard-flying bird. Eventually he'll come back to you and you can resume your hunt. If you have not done a lot of upland work with your dog, this is not the time for heavy discipline with the remote collar. Don't use the collar to stop a chase or reinforce Come on a hunt unless you've shot at least a couple dozen birds over your dog. You wouldn't want to do anything to lessen his desire to search and flush. If he hasn't had a good number of positive experiences with flushing upland birds, the message he's be getting from too much discipline is that birds are bad, and that's the last thing you want him to think!

The same thing goes for trailing. Being able to follow a running rooster is a great skill that your dog gets better at with experience. Unfortunately, that rooster often ends up flushing well out of gun range. It is up to you to put the brakes on fast trailing that ends with a bird getting away. However, you can't apply any discipline

When a dog isn't finding birds and starts to lose motivation the first thing he'll do is start plodding.

to this activity until your dog has had lots and lots of success in the uplands. As with chasing, you have to assess his excitement and experience level before leaning on him for simply doing what comes naturally.

At the same time, there is a comfortable, preferred range within which your dog should work. He should hunt at a distance that allows you time to make the shot when a bird flushes. Depending on what type of cover you're in, that could be anywhere from 10 to 25 yards. Most importantly, always keep your dog in sight. If you hunt standing corn it's pretty easy to lose track of your dog. Same goes with cattail sloughs and tall CRP fields. Don't hesitate to put a bell or beeper on your retriever. Pointing dog guys consider them standard equipment and they can make your day a lot less stressful as well. In tall switchgrass, I frequently use a beeper collar set to "locate" mode. It doesn't beep unless I press a transmitter button and I only need to do that if I momentarily lose track of my dog in the heavy cover.

Another neat trick I use with some of my dogs is to train them to respond to the tone that is available on many remote collars. I can train a dog to change quartering directions upon hearing the tone, or I can train him to come back to me. This just about eliminates the need for talking, yelling or whistling, and that's always a good thing when you're trying to get close to upland birds.

Just a reminder: As always, remain keenly aware of wind direction, doing your best to set your young dog up to hunt into the wind! Various wind-direction scenarios were discussed in Chapter 7 if you need to review.

THE PARTY HUNTING FACTOR

Now, this philosophy of letting your dog learn by doing is as much about training as it is about hunting. If you're hunting with buddies, you need to be sure ahead of time that they understand what you're trying to accomplish and that they have the patience for it.

Then there's the issue of hunting with other dogs. Depending on your dog's personality, hunting with a more experienced dog could be good or bad. A common scenario is for a young retriever to simply chase the older dog around in the field trying to get him to play. So you end up with one annoyed dog, some irritated hunting partners and probably not much success. Furthermore, if some birds are flushed and shot, the older dog will probably get to make the retrieve, either because of experience or tenacity, and that doesn't do anything to help your dog learn. I've also seen young dogs simply let the older dog do all the work while waiting for the chance to rush in and make the retrieve. Again, not what you're supposed to be accomplishing. The bottom line is that, while there are instances of a young dog hunting well with others, I prefer to let my dogs learn through experience without any "help" from my buddies' dogs.

Another consideration when hunting with friends is that if another hunter is blowing his whistle a lot your dog could become confused and think he's supposed to keep coming back to you. The best solution for all concerned is to keep some distance between your dog and the rest of the party. Plan this and other ground rules before you hit the field – how many dogs hunting at once, whistles or no whistles, how much ground you are going to try to cover, etc. Sometimes you just have to find a diplomatic way to explain that you and your dog need to hunt by yourselves. After all, you're still trying to develop a reliable, finished retriever, and you've put a lot of time into this project. There's no sense in undoing a bunch of your hard work.

The best solution for all concerned is to keep some distance between your dog and the rest of the party.

STUFF YOU NEED

The list of ways your dog can get injured in the uplands is a long one. Don't simply hope nothing bad happens; plan your trips knowing that yes, somewhere, sometime, you will have to deal with a problem. You have to constantly check your dog for injuries. More than a few times while taking a break I've rolled a dog over only to find that he had a gaping wound on his chest or belly inflicted by barbed wire. In fact, if you spend enough time pheasant hunting, I can just about guarantee that barbed wire is going to mess up an otherwise great day.

A Basic First Aid Kit

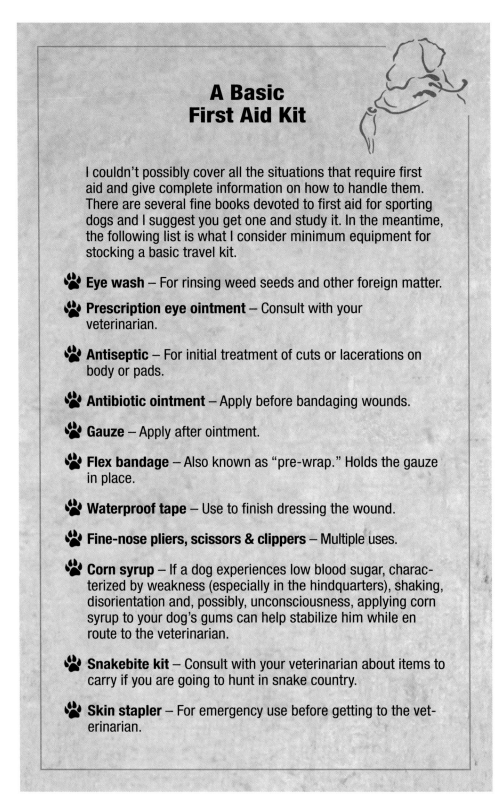

I couldn't possibly cover all the situations that require first aid and give complete information on how to handle them. There are several fine books devoted to first aid for sporting dogs and I suggest you get one and study it. In the meantime, the following list is what I consider minimum equipment for stocking a basic travel kit.

- **Eye wash** – For rinsing weed seeds and other foreign matter.

- **Prescription eye ointment** – Consult with your veterinarian.

- **Antiseptic** – For initial treatment of cuts or lacerations on body or pads.

- **Antibiotic ointment** – Apply before bandaging wounds.

- **Gauze** – Apply after ointment.

- **Flex bandage** – Also known as "pre-wrap." Holds the gauze in place.

- **Waterproof tape** – Use to finish dressing the wound.

- **Fine-nose pliers, scissors & clippers** – Multiple uses.

- **Corn syrup** – If a dog experiences low blood sugar, characterized by weakness (especially in the hindquarters), shaking, disorientation and, possibly, unconsciousness, applying corn syrup to your dog's gums can help stabilize him while en route to the veterinarian.

- **Snakebite kit** – Consult with your veterinarian about items to carry if you are going to hunt in snake country.

- **Skin stapler** – For emergency use before getting to the veterinarian.

Remember when your retriever was a little puppy and I told you to handle his feet and look into his eyes so he got used to it? Well, that kind of stuff really pays off now. You have to constantly check his feet and remove any burrs, sharp seeds or anything else that has gotten into or between the pads. Weed seeds have a way of working their way under the eyelids and causing irritation.

Get a well-stocked first aid kit and make sure it's always available. If you're hours away from a veterinarian, something as simple as a disposable skin stapler could literally save your dog's life. (See the suggested first-aid kit contents list at the end of this chapter.) Also, the first thing you should do upon arriving at your hotel on an out-of-town trip is to look up the name and number of all area veterinarians. Emergencies never happen at convenient times or in convenient places, so knowing how to find someone 24/7 is very important.

No matter how much exercise your dog gets during the off-season, hunting day after day on an extended trip will be taxing. Make sure he gets quality rest time; don't hunt him several hours straight without a break. At night, make sure he doesn't have to burn valuable energy just to stay warm. The zip-on kennel covers that fit over travel crates are incredibly efficient. At the other end of the spectrum, be aware of how devastating warm weather can be to a re-

Use peanut butter to teach your dog to drink from a squirt bottle.

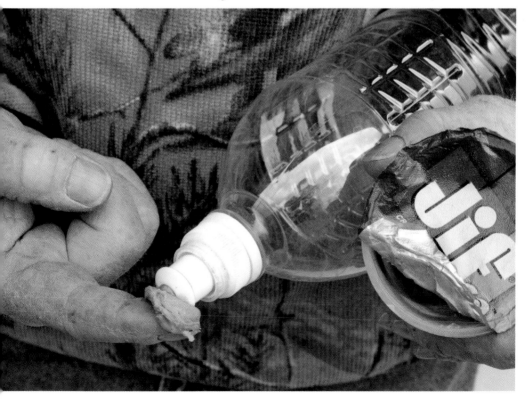

triever. If it's warm, plan short hunts in which you never end up a great distance from your vehicle.

In any weather it's important to carry more water than you think your dog could possibly need. You can't hope you're going to stumble across a pond or stream. Find a water bottle with a squirt top and always make sure it's full before you head out. In fact, carry a couple. If you're hunting with a partner, have him stash another one in his vest too. A neat trick to teach your dog when he's a puppy so he'll always be willing to drink from a squirt bottle is to simply dab some peanut butter on the tip. Do this a few times and he'll always come after the bottle when he sees it. From there it's a simple transition to fill the bottle and get him to drink from it. With this accomplished you don't have to always rely on a water bowl to get your dog to drink.

TRAVEL NOTES

The more you travel with your dog, the better you become at doing so efficiently. Here are just a couple of tips to help you avoid hassles.

If you're going to stay at a hotel be sure you understand their pets policy before you get there. If your retriever is a family dog used to staying in the house you'll want to bring him in the room

SKUNKED! NOW WHAT?

Sooner or later, it's going to happen: Your dog is going to take a hit from an angry skunk. Here's a simple kit you can keep in the truck so you'll always be ready to deal with this aggravating event.

🐾 **Contents:** Two one-gallon jugs of water, a pint of hydrogen peroxide, a box of baking soda and a small bottle of dish soap.

🐾 Rinse your dog with a half-gallon of water. If he was sprayed in the face, rinse his eyes with water and/or saline and apply ointment. To the remaining half-gallon, add the hydrogen peroxide, a quarter-cup of baking soda and a squirt of dish soap. Rub the mixture into the dog's fur and let sit for 15 minutes. Rinse dog with the second gallon. This initial treatment won't remove 100 percent of the odor, but it should make travel bearable until you are able to give him another washing.

with you. Some hotels allow it for free; others charge a small fee. Some ask for a damage deposit, which is only fair. If a hotel clerk says they don't allow dogs, sometimes offering a generous deposit will change their mind.

Flying presents a whole bunch of hurdles. Regulations can vary from one airline to another. There are restrictions regarding temperature at the time of travel. There are health certificate requirements. There are crate-size rules. And there's other stuff that they seem to make up as they go along. My suggestion is to visit the airline's Web site for details about traveling with pets. Then call the airline at the local airport well in advance of the day you are going to travel to see if their requirements are the same as those stated on the Web site. Then, just to be safe, call again right before you head to the airport. It's amazing how many different answers they are capable of giving to the same questions. If you are paranoid and anticipate problems, you'll be less likely to have any.

–13–
TRAINING TO HANDLE

I'm calling this chapter "post-graduate" because, depending on what you expect of your retriever, it might be optional. Handling, as it applies to retriever training, is the ability to direct your dog to various places from a distance. For example, if you send him to retrieve a duck that fell in some tall grass and as he swims he gets off-course, you can handle (or "cast") him right, left, toward or away from you in an effort to guide him closer to the bird. You can even cast your dog back at an angle, if necessary, once he fully understands how to take these directions from you at 50 … 100 … or 150 yards … really any distance from which he can see and hear you. Handling is a great tool to have available, but I'm not talking about it until the very end because everything that came before this is much more important in your dog's first year. After you've gotten through a hunting season, handling is a fun exercise to work on before the next one. And there's no timetable, so you can train at your leisure.

If you use your retriever exclusively for upland hunting, or if you're just an occasional waterfowler, you might not be too concerned with teaching this skill. But if you really enjoy retriever training it's a great way to work with your dog year-round (which you should do anyway) and an enjoyable challenge for both of you.

You will see some people work on these exercises before their dog is a year old. To each his own, but to most hunters this chapter would be considered advanced training. Therefore, be absolutely sure your dog is rock solid on everything you've worked on in previous chapters.

YOU'VE ALREADY LAID THE GROUNDWORK

The platform training you spent so much time on is the cornerstone of handling. What you're really

AFTER THE FIRST SEASON HIGHLIGHTS

You've Already Laid the Ground Work

Introduction to Casting

Perfecting "Back"

Angle Backs

Baseball

Stopping on the Whistle

Wagon Wheel

Running Lines

In "down the line," teach your dog to move from one platform to the next.

working on here is an advanced version of the Place command. Not only will you extend the distances as you send him from one platform to another, but you'lll also train him to go to one of several platforms based on your hand signals.

Keep your dog's enthusiasm up by taking frequent breaks and using lots of fun dummies.

Getting started with handling has much in common with the later stages of Place training. It's a review of the concept that then advances to more challenging commands. Until now, when you sent him to the platform from a short distance, his job was complete when he got there. Now you're going to show him that you may ask him at any time to move again. It starts out simple, but eventually the new place could be in any number of directions from where he is stopped.

You'll need more platforms to get started with the first step, which I call "down the line." Set up four to five platforms in a line, with only three feet or so from one to the next. If you decide to use a more portable type of platform instead of the larger tire platforms described earlier, make sure you get your dog accustomed to them before you work on these drills.

Starting with your dog next to you on one end, command Place while tugging on the leash and giving remote collar stimulus in the form of taps (as opposed to continuous stimulus). These stimulus taps let him know it's time to move, whereas continuous stimulus might give him the wrong message and freeze him. As soon as he gets to the

next platform release the pressure. Let him stay on the platform a few seconds and then repeat, moving toward the next platform. Basically you're walking your dog at heel, and if he's not on a platform he's feeling both remote collar and leash pressure. When you get to the final platform, turn around and go back the other way. After you've done this a few times and you know he understands the concept, leave the leash on but use only remote collar pressure as you move with him from one from one platform to the next. Finally, repeat the drill using a tap on his rear with the heeling stick as the motivation. You're showing him he has to move in the designated direction quickly no matter what type of pressure you apply.

At this stage and as you advance through the handling drills, be sure to take lots of breaks. Handling drills require lots of repetition, so it's important to keep your dog's enthusiasm up with lots of fun dummies at the end of a session.

INTRODUCTION TO CASTING

Now you're ready to start directing your dog from somewhere other than beside you. Start with two platforms six feet apart. Have your dog sit on one platform while you stand in front of him. The other platform is on your right. Hold the leash in your right hand and the heeling stick in your left hand. Now, simply command Place while moving to your right, gesturing to the right with your right arm and guiding your dog to the right platform with a couple taps from the heeling stick. Wait a few seconds and repeat the drill in the opposite direction. This is the first step in teaching your dog to move from side to side, or the "Over" command.

Just as you did in the down the line drill, this next drill is reinforced with taps on the remote collar to get him to move from one platform to the next.

Your dog should pick this up pretty quickly, so now you have to show him what "Back" means. Trade the leash for the check cord because now you'll need to give him more line. After your dog is on the left platform, you simply move way to the left so you and the platforms are in a line. Now command Place again while raising your arm as if you are pushing your dog backwards. Your dog makes the same move he has been, but you are directing him from a different position. Once he's on the far platform, command Place again to get him to move toward you and stop on the near platform.

At this stage and as you advance through the handling drills, be sure to take lots of breaks.

Begin teaching the Over command using two platforms, the leash and the heeling stick.

Once he's on the far platform, command Place again to bring him back to the near platform.

Once he's got
the idea, do the
exercise again
without the
check cord.

PERFECTING "BACK"

Often when you want your dog to go back you will have a preference about whether he turns to his right or to his left before taking off. The direction he turns as he goes away from you will take him a few degrees right or left from straight back. If you are trying to send him to a duck that's, say, 10 degrees to the right of straight back, you would cast him with your right arm. He will turn to the right and head out. Even though he is in fact following your command, he'll naturally drift just a hair to the right and, hopefully, almost run right into the bird. The important thing is that your dog turns right or left depending on which arm you cast him with. He can't be allowed to just randomly turn either way.

Teach this concept using three platforms in a V shape. Your dog is on the platform at the bottom of the V. Another platform sits six feet behind him at a 45-degree angle on the right and another behind him at a 45-degree angle on the left. Stand just a few feet in front of your dog and command Place, raising your right

Your dog should turn left or... right depending on which arm you cast with.

arm and taking an exaggerated step to the right. Make sure you have the check cord on your dog in case you need to guide him, but he should pick up on this without too much difficulty. When he gets to the right platform, wait a few seconds and then call him back to the starting platform. Then repeat the drill to the left.

After a few sessions of this, move the starting platform farther away from the other two, creating a sharper V. The sharper you make it, the less obvious it is which platform he should go to. However, if he's truly taking his cue from you and not running at random, he should make the proper right or left turn, whichever way you send him.

Teach this concept using three platforms in a V shape.

Begin by casting
your dog from
the first platform
to the one on the
right.

ANGLE BACKS

Sometimes you will want to send your dog in a direction that is neither straight back nor straight to the side. Somewhere in between those two extremes is the angle back. When you raise your arm to angle your dog right or left, you basically want to point in the direction of the fall. After many repetitions your dog will be able to distinguish between an angle cast and a straight-over or back cast.

Set up this drill with five platforms laid out in a zig-zag pattern, each about six feet from the next. Place your dog on the first platform and then cast him to the one sitting behind him and to his right. There should be no confusion as to where he thinks he should go because you've already showed him how to make the correct right or left turn, and when he turns to the right he should naturally go the platform nearest him.

When he's on the second platform, step up and past the first platform, effectively blocking him from returning to the place he started. Now give him the Place command while casting your arm toward the left-angled platform. Step into the gap between that platform and the one he just left and give him a Place with a right-angle

Next, step up past the first platform and cast him to the one on the left.

Then, step up again and send him to the next platform.

Repeat this
process in the
other direction

There should be no confusion as to where he thinks he should go because you've already showed him how to make the correct right or left turn, and when he turns to the right he should naturally go the platform nearest him.

cast. Then repeat again with a left-angle cast. Now he should be on the fifth and last platform in your zig-zag setup. Simply walk around until you are facing him and repeat the drills going in the opposite direction.

During this introductory phase, or at any time during these initial handling drills, be ready with the heeling stick and taps on the collar to move him along if he doesn't want to leave the platform. Yes, the platform is a "safe" area, but he has to always understand that moving away is as important as any of his obedience commands.

When your dog really has this down, start your next session with him at heel, sending him to the first platform and then going through the angle drills.

Begin baseball by sending your dog to the pitcher's mound from home plate.

BASEBALL

Retriever trainers have been using "baseball" for decades to introduce dogs to handling from a distance. It's still a popular and effective method today. To teach casting with the baseball method, you need a chunk of ground with very short cover. Set platforms on the pitcher's mound and first, second and third base. The first time you do this drill the distance from the pitcher's mound to each base should only be about 10 feet. You are going to direct him from home plate.

Obviously, you can't start baseball until you're sure your dog understands all the directional signals you've showed him in the previous sections. If you're sure he's ready, go ahead and start your first baseball drill with him sitting beside you at home plate. Looking straight ahead and with your hand just above his head but where he can see it, move your hand toward the pitcher's mound and command Place.

Don't follow any particular order. Mix it up so your dog won't be able to anticipate where you will send him next.

When he's on the pitcher's mound you have the option of sending him right, left or back to each base. Don't follow any particular order. You don't want your dog anticipating which way you will send him. When he gets the close stuff down, start extending the platform distances, perhaps 10 yards at a time. Each time you do this drill set it up in the same place. That way it becomes a real confidence-builder. Give yourself a goal of increasing the distances to each base to about 50 yards.

When you reach the point where your dog is reliably casting to the correct platform every time, put a few training dummies on each one. Now he will run over to the platform and scoop up a dummy. Call him back to you, give lots of praise and then walk him out to the pitcher's mound for his next cast. Eventually, remove the platforms entirely and use dummies only.

Remember, if your dog ever acts like he's confused about which direction he's supposed to be going, or if he's ignoring you and running randomly to whichever platform he wants, shorten up the distances and do some retroactive training. Again, there's no timetable to worry about. Take small steps and make sure your dog always gets it before moving on to a new challenge.

Once he's on the pitcher's mound, send him right, left or back to each base.

STOPPING ON THE WHISTLE

A crucial part of handling is the ability to stop your dog instantly when you need to cast him in a new direction. Therefore you should teach him to stop on a single whistle blast. This is ridiculously easy to teach. When you are walking your dog at heel and come to a stop, simply say Sit and give a light blast on the whistle.

Once he's got the idea, add dummies to increase your dog's enthusiasm.

After several repetitions he'll automatically associate the whistle with sitting.

When working on the baseball drill, begin giving one whistle blast each time he reaches a platform. You can reinforce the command with the remote collar. I suggest doing this reinforcing in the yard to be sure he gets it before you start tying it in with patterning drills.

WAGON WHEEL

Another basic but beneficial drill is the wagon wheel. This consists of four platforms situated at the noon, 3-, 6- and 9-o'clock positions. You and your dog are in the center and each platform is only six feet or so away. This is a great exercise to make sure your dog is moving at heel with you as you turn to face a platform and then send him to it. As noted to earlier, you are sending him by holding your hand above and out in front of his head, and then moving it slightly in the direction you want to send him. The hand signal and his name together get him moving, similar to the way you did things during the steadiness drills in Chapter 11.

When your dog is reliably turning with you and going to the correct platform each time, go ahead and move them back several yards. When he is reliably going to the correct platform each time

In the wagon wheel drill, send your dog from the heel position to each platform.

you can finally replace the platforms with training dummies just like you did during baseball training.

And finally, when your dog is full of confidence and running hard every time, go ahead and get rid of the platforms. Seeing the dummy pile is enough of a visual cue to keep him going. Eventually you can run your drills in some short cover. If you've done lots of repetitions and he is confident that there will be a dummy in his path at some point, he should run with plenty of enthusiasm. Every now and then use fresh-killed birds to really ramp up his excitement level.

Once your dog goes to the correct platform each time, replace the platforms with training dummies and repeat the drill.

RUNNING LINES

The wagon wheel exercises got your dog tuned up for running blind retrieves, and it shouldn't be terribly difficult to get him to run short distances in a straight line even if he can't see the bird. Now you're ready to work on getting him to run long distances toward a hidden bird. This starts out with a very simple routine. Load up a bucket with several dummies and walk out into a field of very short grass with your dog at heel. Set down the bucket and take out the dummies, dropping them in front of the bucket while your dog watches.

Now, go back about 20 yards or so and send him to pick up the dummies one at a time. This is the time to introduce the words "dead bird," which becomes a cue to tell him he's going to be running a line. You have been using your dog's name to release him to make a retrieve. Now add in the Back command with the goal of transitioning to Back alone for blind retrieves. Say Back when you want to send him. He probably won't move because he hasn't heard this word yet. So say Back and then his name. Eventually you will be able to drop his name, because after several repetitions he will understand what Back means.

Use real birds in these exercises to keep your dog focused and eager to run.

To complete this signal training, move your baseball pattern from your yard to a larger area.

Begin with platforms at shorter distances, and show your dog each platform prior to running the drill.

Advance through the drill by increasing the distance out to the platforms.

Once your dog is consistent with the signals on land, move the game to the water. Start short and work towards longer distances.